Dedicated to Hope, Felicinda, Craig, Denise
& to all of my guides, angels and mentors
that have assisted in opening a space of higher
awareness in my life.

# *3,6,9* Secrets

**How to Be, Have, and Create with All the Abundance in the Universe**

Nathan Minnehan

It's MINE.

It's OUT THERE.

I DESERVE IT.

I HAVE A PURPOSE FOR IT.

AND THAT PURPOSE

WILL HELP

AND HEAL

THE WORLD.

AMEN.

*(say this over and over all day long until what you see in here, manifests out there...)*

# *3,6,9* Secrets

**How to Be, Have, and Create with All the Abundance in the Universe**

**By Nathan Minnehan**

**ISBN:** 979-8-950444-01-2

**Published by:** AUTHOR TO BE

**An imprint of:**

Inspiration On Tap

2336 SE Ocean Blvd #222

Stuart, FL 34996

# Foreword

"To see a World in a Grain of Sand
And a Heaven in a Wild Flower
Hold Infinity in the palm of your hand
And Eternity in an hour"

**-William Blake**

For many years I have lived with a conscious connection between what I thought, what I saw, and what happened. In life there are many signs. Often it takes believing to see them. On a basic level much of the population of the intellectual world believes in some form of a higher power. Depending on their depth and persuasion that higher power can simply be accepted and understood without question. To live in this way is healthy in that it honors our higher nature as spiritual creatures. But to truly wield the tools of a spiritual warrior one must throw off the bowlines, burn the ships, and sail away from any safe harbor.

To become a warrior of the light is to say, I accept this life in its fullest, and I'm going to live it to the core. Or in the words of Thoreau, "I'm going to suck out all of the marrow of life so that when I come to die not discover that I had not lived."

Life happens in layers, and before we know it we are landscapers of our own realities. We in fact plant the seeds that grow into the tree or weeds that either must be tended to or plucked.

In my modest age of 34 I have come to find that life is not all butterflies and rainbows, however I have learned that it can be. To consistently peel back the layers of perception, and to become aware of how we and everything around us comes to be is to undergo the path within, to walk the path toward and of enlightenment.

To acknowledge the light, to honor it, and to move with it.

Life is full of forces; love, joy, pain, excitement, desperation, exaltation, elation, exhaustion, sorrow, shame, to name a few.

These forces are often labeled as emotions, but on an energetic level they are indeed forces. And in a society that thrives off of labeling problems and selling ready made solutions, we must not forget what is and will always be true. That we have the power. For the word begins with us. When we open our mouths to speak, we have the power. To say, I am… fill in the blank. Every thought begins in the mind, and a thought thunk closest to the mind of the divine will surely burn with the greatest light; the most energetically long lasting, for it will exist outside of time for anything brought so close to the divine for a moment moves into the eternal and from there it is forever brought into the divine rhythm.

We are now living in the most advanced and at the same time inundated time in all of history.

With so much noise we could easily become hypnotized into living a life that feels dull or seems lackluster. For if comparison is the thief of joy then we are all living in the robbers den from sun up to sun down as we stare into our black mirrors day in and day out.

What I am offering here is a set of tools. A box if you will of concepts that have somehow come to find me over the years on my path. I wish you a safe journey, but not too safe. A good life, but not too rich. A proud history but not overly prideful. For to forgo pain is to miss out on process. And process is where we become submerged in the realm of the forms, and where our inner strength is strengthened as we are brought closer to the mind of the divine in our most and dearest moments. In our most humble of times. That is when we must in the words of Gladiator, rise and rise again, until lambs become lions.

> ***Please take everything with a grain of salt, and remember that not all salt is for you, for you are already that salt you seek.***

This forward was written at 9:28 EST in the Times Square building in Rochester, NY on August 22nd, 2023. It's a beautiful sunny day and I'm looking out the window on the ninth floor. The rest of this text was written in Portugal, Brasil, London, and up in the air on a plane. While this is currently me writing and typing, you'll notice that once you move into the definitions portion of the text that much was written with the assistance of AI. While I do honor the craft of my own written word, much of this book has been inspired from a place of organizing thought schools under one cover. To be a jumping off place toward higher consciousness, and a springboard for all who read it. May it propel you and your magical life to new heights and braver trajectories.

In friendship I extend my right hand, and offer you my best.

Sincerely yours,

**-Nathan Minnehan**

P.S. As I looked up at the time when I finished typing and editing, the clock on my computer screen read: 9:36 AM. There are only coincidences. You choose.

# Enter:

FLOW state of mind written in Porto, Portugal in the spring of 2023:

In Order to have everything we desire we must first *have it.* Have it and hold it in our mind's eye. During the waking and resting of each day. We must rest inside of a deep awareness, and wake up inside of the deep awareness. We must look for ways to bring what we are *having* closer and closer into our mind's nest. As if our mind had arms to hug our vision. We must be willing, open, and clear about how we are to hug our clear having and have it.

We must be absolutely clear about what it is so that when it shows up we know how to reach out and grab it. This is the secret. We are quantum worlds away from our dreams and desires downloading into the here and now and pretty soon you'll be inside of what you've been having and not even recall that this is what you had first had before you were currently experiencing it in the physical.

Imagine a very dry and dense piece of wood. Now imagine placing it in a pond. And letting it sit. Let it steep. You "having" your vision is equivalent to the log steeping over time until it is quite definitely waterlogged and the board is now heavier than ever. This is how a vision manifests. It takes time to seep in. But seep into where? Into the physical reality?

Yes but first somewhere else. First into the second most powerful mind in the universe. That is the subconscious mind. The first most powerful being the mind of God and the third most powerful being our conscious mind, and the 4th most powerful being the mastermind. The gathering of minds for a common purpose which creates the mastermind through which the gathered conscious mind benefits.

If we can learn how to effectively tap into and create our lives by passing our "having" deep into the subconscious mind and hug it so closely to us then the manifesting of it in our physical realities is imminent. It will first manifest in the things you see around you. And held long enough your eyes will one day open and it will be there. Right in front of you.

*A Brief Introduction to Nathan…*

# *Saint Germain des pres cafe volume 5*

*"Though we are told to mourn it we must know it was a noble sound…*

*as we gather here to mourn the passing of a noble sound, we should take the pains to remember something..*

*There are some of us that do not accept the dreams of dragons as their own no matter how grand the dragons might say they are…*

*yes there are some who refuse to drop the candle even when pushed into a dark cave and locked there behind a stone.*

*There is you must recall a kind of serious study that will give you the confidence to strike your match to the mighty weak that will illuminate yet another portion of the darkness. You must be willing to accept the fact that pain is a part of the process of revelation…*

*You have to be willing to take the field and stay on the field the way that Duke stayed on the road. Out there somewhere are the kind of people who do not accept the premature autopsy of a noble art form. These are the ones who follow in the footsteps of the gifted and the disciplined who have been deeply hurt but not discouraged, who have been frightened but have not forgotten how to be brave, who revel in the company of their friends and sweethearts but are willing to face the loneliness that is demanded of mastery."*

I can still hear this music playing in my apartment up on the seventh floor in Chicago overlooking Lake Michigan. I was in my mid twenties and punching, cutting, and stitching leather journals rigorously while dancing and zenning out from early dawn until moonlight crested my forehead. Each and every nook and crevice of my apartment was made by me. I built the whole thing. It looked and felt like the inside of a ship, and easily reminisced of a treehouse out of a movie. It took me two years to build and most of that time I spent alone. Looking, dreaming, gazing, and imagining what I would do with each corner. From floor to ceiling my 450 square foot apartment was transformed and doubled in space through my labyrinth of lofts, and don't forget my table on pulleys and sailing winches that literally tied off to a boat cleat to stay up. I can't make this up even if I tried. Have a gander and go on youtube. Type in Nathan Minnehan, ideas that transform… that's the place. That's my apartment. And yes, believe it or not, that's me. Don't believe it? Can't believe it? Won't believe it?

I can hear the voice in your head now… What happened? Well, the short answer is… a magic trick. The longer answer, and the theme of this entire book is, a transformation. More specifically, an implementation of many of the laws of transformation at their finest. That's what happened. And now, and even then I feel as I have always felt, that it is my job here and now on this planet and in this space to bring to surface the rules, laws, and formulas for this and for all forms of transformation. Many of us look to coaches, which are amazing messengers, but we need only know and implement the laws of transformation, and soon, the transformation will happen.

It starts with an inkling… a deep seated and rooted itch. A feeling of knowing that you are meant to discover something, do something, birth something, manifest something. It all happens once you create the space for it to happen, and that is what we will soon discover as one of the many laws of transformation, is indeed the law of space.

The law of space dictates that in a clear space anything and everything is possible. Move to a clear space and anything and everything that is possible will be possible to and through you.

It's up to us to make space for transformation to occur, happen, become, allow, and flourish.

To become meta-physically and meta-mentally and meta-spiritually conscious and connected is key. And the key is to become the key. To abolish all space between what you're dreaming + knowing + believing + thinking and receiving. You have to become the channel for that which you desire, and the clearest and fastest way to do this is to become / find / discover the angle or the angel that will guide

→ lead the way.

Have you ever noticed the strength of an angled wall? For instance in present 2023 my apartment in Portugal has an angled wall and no matter what you do, you cannot change the angle because it is pitched. And to say that it is pitched to to say that it has a certain tone, angle, and vibration. And to see, have, and understand all of those things is to understand what is at the crux of this next becoming. Of this next you —niverse. The UNIVERSE is YOU-NIVERSE. It's you! All of it. Everything you see, hear, touch, smell, want, desire; all of it!

It's intelligent. It's intelligent becoming, and it's all around you!

The universe is presently dreaming through my fingertips touching these keys writing this message and reaching your eyes and fingertips on this here page. It is dreaming that the right people, the chosen people receive, integrate and take on the truths here in this message. And that they take them on with urgency as I have written this book. Or rather that the book has been downloaded… in the spirit of and from the stars as they and I have aligned and we are here now on this page speaking, dreaming and believing in you and your journey. You and your message, you and your calling; it's all here, it's all ready and it's all now.

The answer to every question you have ever asked has just been answered, you just have to read it again!

You have all of the answers right now inside of you. You know what's coming, what's happening, and what's real! You know it because it's in you! It's happening right now out over the clearing. The opening that you can't see but in your mind's eye.. It is there that it is happening. And your mind is infinite is it not? Does it not live on? If not in your own then in all other minds from now on until the end of time, which has no end? Has no beginning and has no in between. It is all here and now and this is the conundrum that each and every human being is born to seesaw until hopefully one day he or she finds the illumination loophole and begins to realize that we are here for one reason and one reason only....

To CREATE.

We are creators and co-creators of our reality. We are the masters of our fate and the captains of our souls. For one reason and one reason only... Because we THINK!

It is us! We, you and I, us, that are going to the moon and back, for us! And it's up to us to discover the forces and processes that will take us there.

One such force and the origin of all force is the battery pack you'll be pondering to bring you wherever you want to go… and that my friends… is LOVE.

LOVE LOVE LOVE… there's nothing you can do that can't be done, nothing you can sing that can't be sung, nothing you can…

YES, the Beatles knew it! All you need is LOVE.

But I would amend that statement and say ALL YOU NEED IS TO LOVE …

And in there is the great secret. We must begin to love all beings, and all people. Even the bad people. Jesus says to love your enemies and the reason why is simply because of the laws of love. Yes another law of transformation..

The Law of LOVE.

All things are to be loved so that they can be accepted, processed, transmuted and transformed or created.

LOVE = CREATION BECOMING

In order to create we must love. And it's not that we MUST, but that we may and thank God that we can!!!

Do not imagine a universe without love! Oh my goodness, you just did, and isn't it sad! No no no, blow it up, destroy, get rid of it…

That's right. We must all allow ourselves to watch our language. Not like our mothers would say not to swear, not at all.. But rather that it would behoove us to begin to take seriously the words that we say as they craft and convey what it is that we want , want it or not, to the subconscious mind….

Law of blow … Law of Flow … Law of Faux

This is one law.. And this law states that all reality is either created or destroyed. And it is in the understanding of this law that all things change.

Take for instance a chalkboard. Draw a picture of a naked woman on it. Now quickly erase it. What just happened? Did you feel aroused? Change the picture and draw a naked man. Whatever your preference is. Does the feeling of becoming aroused change anything?

Well, ask yourself this, have you ever fallen in love with someone or something or the idea of something. Talked about it for days, weeks, months, and years?

Well then you indeed know that when you

feel something something happens, and it begins to happen more and faster as you begin to know, understand and wield the laws of transformation in your life / picture / vortex.

As you can see there's a lot of information spilling out in between my ranting here.. I wasn't just building lofts and crafting leather notebooks in that chicago apartment… I was absorbing, dreaming, and envisioning my higher self taking the wheel and steering me toward the life of my dreams.

What dreams? Well the ones on my vision board of course. The same vision board that is on the wall in each one of my apartments and my offices ten years later. And on the glasses cloth that comes with my brand's sunglasses.

Yes… This is not fantasy… whoops! Made you think. Good, we're getting somewhere.

We are all living in an Alice in Wonderland world, it's just that some of us are more aware of how to construct, create and destroy the walls wherever they appear.

It's up to us to bring each other up to speed. To increase our velocity is to increase our speed of manifestation which is to simply turn the dial … change the channel… or as I like to say, swim into a new you.. Move into a higher notion, let go in a bigger and fuller way. Make way for the amazing you to become and to appear.

It's here and now that everything happens and so it's here and now that YOU HAPPEN because this YOU-NIVERSE is all YOU and it's all happening now simultaneously all around you.

So… may I?

As I pour you a cup of coffee from my french press in the boat house loft apartment in Chicago.

May I? I'm asking once again..

For that's not coffee and we're not in Chicago, or are we?

Reality can be respelled.. REAL - I - TY

Let's use English and Czech to solve this equation.

REAL - English word meaning of substance.
I - English word meaning "me" or "you" in this case.
TY - Czech word meaning "you".

So.. REAL YOU. Reality is REAL YOU.

Now let's solve another word equation.

FANTASY.

Fan - someone fond of someone, or a spinning object, or to move in a spinning out way.

TA - Czech article meaning "that one"

SY - sounds like "see" in English meaning to view

Now FANTASY can be solved as FAN TO SEE ...

So.. REAL YOU and FAN TO SEE...

Switch it around and you have FAN TO SEE REAL YOU.

The YOU-NIVERSE is a FAN TO SEE REAL YOU.

Who else in your life is a FAN TO SEE THE REAL YOU?

Hmmm your mother, your father, your

grandma and grandpa, your special aunt, your special uncle. That one maybe one real friend. That really loves you and wants the best for you. Those real fans. They all love you.

And again at the root of this equation is LOVE.

And so as the Beatles began and as we are amending.. All YOU NEED IS TO LOVE.

This is where our story starts. In this bizarre and stranger than fiction story of real life that I am telling you right now. Because life is too short to miss the truth. We must make the truth and the pursuit and love of it as the core of our inner beings.

I love to listen to books on tape, audible, cd, you name it! Most of them are self improvement, metaphysical, spiritual, biographies, parables, and exceptional novels like the Fountainhead or Shantaram… Or the Alchemist.. But that's not a novel.. That's a parable.

Which allows me / us to solve this word equation. PARABLE.

PAR - in this case we'll go with the sound…. Pair / to connect / or a collection of two.

ABLE - able to … allowable…

So… ABLE TO PAIR.

A parable is ABLE TO PAIR with your REAL YOU or reality.

The and the parable presents itself as one of those energy packs that when tapped, turned on, and transformed can move anything. Mountains, pyramids, and primarily worlds..

To shape and to shift. And so we have another

law…

The Law of Shaping and Shifting..

The law of shaping and shifting states that we must make use of our powers to shape and to shift by literally shaping and shifting.

To shape a thing outside is to in-directly shape a thing inside.

Like a book… you hold it, you carry it, you fold it, you fondle it… and little by little you absorb something in the examining of the contents and that something makes its way into something else that you are already doing and that something could in fact be the key to really solving and creating with a fuller force, a stronger conviction, and a greater view.

Speaking of view…

Come on over here… Do you see that? See what, you might be asking. Do you not see it?

See what, you might be insisting…

Ah… there's the rub. That place we just pointed to, touched, felt, and either stirred from toward or in, that's the magic mirror. That's the place where everything appears, happens, is created, destroyed, loved, lost, gained, or forgotten. That's the mystery of the mind, and inside the mind is the mystery of life.

It is not to be solved but pondered. And in pondering created. And in creating, *loved.*

ALL YOU NEED IS TO LOVE.

# THE 3,6,9 FACULTY

The development of a higher awareness and the ability to implement tools of higher self into everyday life for the living of life in an effortless state of enlightenment, connected to synchronicities that present themselves, living with our higher faculties and guidance systems in place to reach our highest potentials as human beings and spiritual beings of light for the helping and healing of the world, planet, and mankind. To live fully in the *Fifth Dimension.*

# GLOSSARY OF 3,6,9 SECRETS' TERMINOLOGIES

Living your life in the fifth dimension *(What is the fifth dimension)*
Laws of vibration
Laws of transformation
Laws of intention
Laws of germination
Laws of attraction
Laws of manifestation

The law of Quantum physics
The law of Quantum Mechanics
The law of Quantum Leaping

# Nikola Tesla's 3, 6, 9 Number sequence

# PART 1

# Important Terms & Concepts

# Laws of Vibration

The Kybalion is a book that was published in the early 20th century, which is said to be a compilation of ancient Hermetic teachings. Among the many ideas presented in this book are the seven laws of vibration, which are fundamental principles that govern the universe. These laws are said to apply to everything in existence, from the smallest subatomic particles to the largest galaxies. In this essay, we will discuss each of the laws of vibration as presented in the Kybalion.

The first law of vibration is the law of mentalism. This law states that everything in the universe is created by the mind. In other words, all of the physical objects and phenomena that we observe are the result of mental processes. This law suggests that the universe is a product of the cosmic mind, and that everything is interconnected and interdependent.

The second law of vibration is the law of correspondence. This law states that there is a correspondence between the physical and mental planes of existence. In other words, what happens in the physical world has a corresponding effect on the mental world, and vice versa. This law suggests that the mind and body are not separate entities, but are intimately connected.

The third law of vibration is the law of vibration. This law states that everything in the universe is in a constant state of vibration. This includes both the physical and mental planes of existence. This law suggests that everything is energy, and that all energy vibrates at different frequencies.

The fourth law of vibration is the law of polarity. This law states that everything in the universe has two opposite poles, and that these poles are necessary for the existence of the thing. For example, light cannot exist without darkness, and hot cannot exist without cold. This law suggests that everything in the universe is balanced and that there is a natural duality to everything.

The fifth law of vibration is the law of rhythm. This law states that everything in the universe is in a constant state of motion, and that this motion occurs in cycles. This law suggests that everything has a natural rhythm or pattern, and that these patterns repeat themselves over time.

The sixth law of vibration is the law of cause and effect. This law states that everything in the universe is connected, and that every action has a corresponding reaction. This law suggests that everything we do has an impact on the world around us, and that we are responsible for our own actions.

The seventh law of vibration is the law of gender. This law states that everything in the universe has a masculine and feminine aspect, and that these aspects are necessary for creation to occur. This law suggests that everything in the universe is constantly creating and evolving, and that this process is driven by the interplay of masculine and feminine forces.

Overall, the laws of vibration put forth by the Kybalion provide a comprehensive framework for understanding the nature of the universe. These laws suggest that everything in the universe is interconnected and interdependent, and that everything is constantly evolving and changing. By studying and applying these laws, we can gain a deeper understanding of ourselves and our place in the world, and we can work to create a more harmonious and balanced existence for ourselves and for all beings.

# *Poetic Recap*

*In the tapestry of life, a truth we find, The laws of vibration, both subtle and kind. From the cosmos above to the earth below, Vibrations connect us, in constant flow.*
*Invisible waves, a cosmic ballet, Vibrations set the world in motion's sway. From atoms to galaxies, all is in tune, Resonating rhythms, from night to noon.*

*Harmony's secret, vibrations confess, In music's sweet notes, they gently caress. Strings and voices, in symphony unite, Vibrations create melodies, pure and bright.*

*In nature's embrace, a wondrous display,*

*Vibrations dictate how creatures convey. From chirping of birds to the roar of the sea, Vibrations tell stories, in every decree.*

*In stillness, they linger, a tranquil refrain, Yet in movement, they rise like a hurricane. A fluttering leaf, a pendulum's swing, Vibrations are life's voice, a universal thing.*

*In healing's embrace, vibrations restore, They mend the spirit, the body, and more. Resonant frequencies, a soothing balm, Vibrations bring solace, they bring us calm.*
*In the realm of science, vibrations define, The laws of the universe, their design. From light's spectrum to sound's gentle thrum, Vibrations unveil secrets, one by one.*

*Energy's essence, vibrations convey, Transforming matter in their own unique way. From potential to kinetic, they transmute, Vibrations create, they never dispute.*

*So, let us honor the laws of vibration, In this grand cosmic orchestration. For in every heartbeat, in every song, Vibrations guide us, and to them, we belong.*

*In the symphony of life, we find our place, Embracing vibrations, with grace and embrace. In their rhythm, we discover our sensation, Bound to the laws of divine vibration.*

# Laws of Transformation

The laws of transformation refer to a set of principles that describe how energy and matter can be transformed from one form to another. These laws are essential in physics, chemistry, and engineering, and they govern the behavior of all physical systems. In this article, we will discuss the three laws of transformation in detail and provide examples of how they apply in various contexts.

## First Law of Transformation: The Law of Conservation of Energy

The first law of transformation states that energy cannot be created or destroyed, only transformed from one form to another. This principle is also known as the law of conservation of energy. It implies that the total amount of energy in a closed system remains constant, although it can be transformed from one form to another.

For example, when we burn wood, the chemical energy stored in the wood is converted into thermal energy, which can be used to heat a room. However, the total amount of energy in the system remains constant, and no energy is created or destroyed.

## Second Law of Transformation: The Law of Entropy

The second law of transformation is known as the law of entropy. It states that in any energy transformation process, the total amount of disorder or randomness (entropy) in the system increases. This means that energy tends to flow from a concentrated form to a dispersed form, and the amount of useful energy available to do work decreases over time.

For example, when we burn gasoline in an

engine, the chemical energy stored in the fuel is converted into mechanical energy, which can be used to move a car. However, during the transformation process, some of the energy is lost as heat, sound, and friction. This loss of useful energy increases the disorder in the system, making it less efficient.

**Third Law of Transformation:
The Law of Conservation of Mass**

The third law of transformation is the law of conservation of mass. It states that in any physical or chemical transformation process, the total mass of the system remains constant. This means that matter cannot be created or destroyed, only transformed from one form to another.

For example, when we burn wood, the mass of the wood is converted into ash, smoke, and gases. However, the total mass of the system remains constant, and no matter is created or destroyed.

## Applications of the Laws of Transformation

The laws of transformation have numerous applications in various fields. In physics, they are used to describe the behavior of energy in different systems, such as heat engines, electrical circuits, and thermodynamic systems. In chemistry, they are used to understand the behavior of chemical reactions, including combustion, oxidation, and reduction.

In engineering, the laws of transformation are used to design and optimize energy conversion systems, such as engines, turbines, and generators. They are also used to improve the efficiency of energy storage and transmission systems, such as batteries, capacitors, and power grids.

## Conclusion

The laws of transformation are fundamental principles that govern the behavior of energy and matter in different systems. The law of conservation of energy states that energy cannot be created or destroyed, only transformed from one form to another. The law of entropy states that the total amount of disorder or randomness in the system increases over time. The law of conservation of mass states that matter cannot be created or destroyed, only transformed from one form to another. These laws have numerous applications in physics, chemistry, and engineering, and they are essential for understanding the behavior of physical systems.

# // More on Laws of Transformation as they apply to personal growth and travel //

Transforming your life through intentional travel, learning a new language, and immersing yourself in a different culture can be a profoundly enriching and health-enhancing experience. This holistic approach to personal growth offers a unique opportunity to expand your horizons, challenge your comfort zone, and develop a more profound understanding of the world and yourself.

The Power of Intentional Travel: Intentional travel goes beyond mere sightseeing. It involves setting clear goals and purposes for your journey, whether it's to seek adventure, foster personal growth, or cultivate meaningful connections. By approaching travel with intention, you create a focused mindset that directs your experiences toward self-discovery and transformation. Each destination becomes a canvas for exploration and learning, as you seek out activities, interactions, and environments that align with your objectives.

Intentional travel also encourages mindfulness and presence. When you're fully engaged in your experiences and attentive to the details of a new place, you create lasting memories and connections. This heightened awareness can lead to a deeper appreciation of life's intricacies and a greater sense of gratitude.

Unlocking a New World Through Language: Learning a new language is akin to opening a door to a world of possibilities. It not only facilitates communication but also provides insights into different cultures, thought patterns, and perspectives. The process of language acquisition stimulates cognitive function, enhancing memory, problem-solving skills, and multitasking abilities. As you navigate the intricacies of grammar, vocabulary, and pronunciation, you exercise your brain, promoting mental agility and resilience.

Moreover, speaking a foreign language can establish connections with people from diverse backgrounds, fostering empathy and cultural understanding. When you communicate in someone else's native tongue, you bridge linguistic and cultural gaps, demonstrating respect and appreciation for their heritage. This exchange of languages can lead to friendships and collaborations that transcend borders.

Embracing Cultural Immersion: Immersing yourself in a new culture allows you to step out of your comfort zone and embrace unfamiliar customs, traditions, and ways of life. This process encourages adaptability and resilience as you navigate new social norms and experiences. As you interact with locals, you gain insights into their worldviews and gain a broader perspective on humanity's rich tapestry.

Cultural immersion also challenges preconceptions and biases, fostering a more open-minded and inclusive outlook. Exposure to different beliefs and values prompts self-reflection and encourages personal growth. By confronting your assumptions, you become more receptive to diverse viewpoints, fostering a deeper sense of empathy and connection with others.

The Health Benefits of Transformative Travel: Engaging in intentional travel, language learning, and cultural immersion not only enriches your mind and soul but also offers numerous health benefits:

Stress Reduction: Stepping away from your routine and immersing yourself in a new environment can reduce stress levels and promote relaxation. Exposure to new experiences and cultures can shift your focus away from daily worries, allowing your mind to unwind.

Cognitive Stimulation: Language learning and cultural immersion challenge your brain, stimulating neural pathways and cognitive functions. This mental exercise can help stave off cognitive decline and enhance memory and problem-solving skills.

Enhanced Creativity: Experiencing different cultures and perspectives can spark your creativity by exposing you to new art forms, music, cuisine, and ways of thinking. These creative stimuli can inspire you to approach challenges in novel ways.

Boosted Confidence: Navigating unfamiliar environments, learning a new language, and successfully adapting to different cultures can significantly boost your self-confidence and self-esteem. Each achievement becomes a testament to your adaptability and resilience.

Personal Growth: Transformative travel encourages self-discovery and personal growth. By stepping outside your comfort zone, you confront limitations and fears, paving the way for enhanced self-awareness and personal development.

Cultural Sensitivity: Embracing new cultures fosters cultural sensitivity and empathy. Developing a broader perspective on global issues and diverse communities can lead to more meaningful connections and a heightened sense of interconnectedness.

Well-being and Happiness: Immersing yourself in enriching experiences and engaging with new people can lead to increased feelings of happiness and overall well-being. The positive emotions associated with transformative travel contribute to a more fulfilling and balanced life.

In conclusion, transforming your life through intentional travel, learning a new language, and immersing yourself in a new culture can lead to profound personal growth and enhanced well-being. By setting clear intentions, exploring different languages, and embracing cultural diversity, you open doors to new perspectives, greater empathy, and a deeper understanding of the world. This transformative journey not only enriches your mind and soul but also brings about positive changes in your cognitive abilities, emotional well-being, and overall quality of life.

## *Poetic Recap*

*In the crucible of time, where change does reign, Lies the essence of life, in its ceaseless gain. The laws of transformation, they silently guide, As the world evolves, with every tide.*

*From seed to sapling, a metamorphosis grand, In nature's realm, where life's patterns expand. A caterpillar's cocoon, a butterfly's flight, Transformation's magic, in the softest light.*

*In the depths of the Earth, where rocks do churn, Molten fires beneath, where new worlds burn. The laws of transformation, forging stones anew, From magma's embrace, to the skies so blue.*

*In human hearts, where emotions ignite, Transformation's journey, from darkness to light. From sorrow to joy, from despair to hope, These laws of change, help humanity cope. In science's domain, where atoms collide, Transforming elements, on this cosmic ride. Nuclear reactions, in stars they perform, The laws of transformation, where galaxies swarm. In society's tapestry, a culture's birth, Transformation's whispers, as old norms unearth. From tradition to progress, a continuous theme, The laws of transformation, a society's dream.*

*In self-discovery, a personal quest, Transformation unfolds, in our heart's bequest. From ignorance to wisdom, we journey within, These laws of growth, they cleanse our soul's sin. From the seasons that shift, to the moon's wax and wane, In the laws of transformation, there's wisdom to gain. For change is the essence, the universe's refrain, A dance of creation, from loss to regain.*

*Embrace these laws, let them be your guide, As you navigate life's ever-changing tide. In transformation's embrace, find strength and grace, For in the laws of change, life finds its place.*

# Laws of Intention

Laws and the power of intention are two interconnected concepts that have significant impact on the way we live our lives. The laws of the universe, such as the law of attraction, state that the energy we put out into the world will be reflected back to us in some way. The power of intention, on the other hand, refers to the ability to consciously direct our thoughts and actions towards a specific outcome.

The law of attraction is perhaps the most well-known law that governs our universe. Simply put, it states that like attracts like. This means that the energy we put out into the world, whether it be positive or negative, will attract similar energy back to us. This is often referred to as the "vibration" we emit. When we are in a positive state of mind, we are said to be emitting a high vibration, which attracts positive experiences and people into our lives. Conversely, when we are in a negative state of mind, we emit a low vibration, which attracts negative experiences and people.

The power of intention is closely related to the law of attraction. In essence, it is the ability to focus our thoughts and actions on a specific outcome. When we set an intention, we are consciously directing our energy towards a desired outcome. This can be applied to any aspect of our lives, from personal goals to professional aspirations. By setting clear intentions, we are able to align our thoughts and actions with our goals, and thereby increase our chances of success.

It's important to note that the power of intention is not a magic pill that will guarantee success in all our endeavors. Rather, it is a tool that we can use to help us achieve our goals. By setting clear intentions and aligning our thoughts and actions with our goals, we are creating a positive momentum that will help us move towards success. However, it is still up to us to put in the necessary effort and take action towards our goals.

The power of intention can be applied in a variety of ways. For example, it can be used to improve our relationships with others. By setting an intention to be more patient, kind, and understanding, we can improve our interactions with others and create more positive experiences. It can also be used to improve our own personal growth and development. By setting an intention to learn new skills or overcome personal challenges, we can take steps towards becoming the best version of ourselves.

In order to harness the power of intention, it's important to cultivate a positive mindset.

This means focusing on the good in our lives, rather than dwelling on the negative. It also means being mindful of our thoughts and feelings, and intentionally directing them towards positive outcomes. By doing so, we are able to create a positive energy that will attract more positive experiences into our lives.

In conclusion, the laws and the power of intention are two powerful concepts that can greatly impact our lives. By understanding and applying these principles, we can create a more positive and fulfilling life for ourselves. Whether it's setting intentions for personal growth, career success, or improved relationships, the power of intention is a tool that can help us achieve our goals and create a life that we truly desire.

# *Poetic Recap*

*In the realm of dreams, where hopes take flight, Reside the laws of intention, radiant and bright. A force unseen, yet profound and true, Guiding our desires, in all that we pursue.*

*With intention's spark, we set our course, A beacon in the night, a potent force. In the chambers of the heart, it takes its hold, The power to shape stories, both young and old.*

*In the realm of creation, intention ignites, The universe listens to our heartfelt insights. With clarity and purpose, we draw it near, The dreams we envision, with every sincere tear.*

*In intention's embrace, we summon our might, To carve our destiny, in the fabric of light. With thoughts and actions, aligned and pure, We manifest our visions, serene and sure.*

*Yet intention, a double-edged sword, Can sow discord, or bring accord. With ego's desires, it can lead astray, But with love and compassion, it'll light the way.*

*In the grand design, intention weaves, A tapestry of stories, where every heart believes. A resonance with purpose, a cosmic connection, Intention shapes our world, with profound reflection.*

*With gratitude and intention, we find our grace, Transforming our journey, in this sacred space. In the laws of intention, we discover the key, To unlock our potential, and truly be free.*

*So, let your intentions be noble and bright, A guiding star in the darkest of night. With a heart full of love, let your dreams take flight,*

*For in the laws of intention, you'll find your light.*

## Laws of Germination

Germination is the process by which a seed sprouts into a new plant. This process is governed by natural laws that have been refined over millions of years of evolution. Understanding these laws can help us better understand the process of germination and, more broadly, the principles of success in life.

The first natural law of germination is that a seed must be in the right environment to sprout. This means that it needs the right combination of moisture, temperature, and nutrients to activate the dormant seed embryo. If any of these factors are not optimal, the seed may not sprout at all, or it may take much longer to do so.

Similarly, in life, success often depends on being in the right environment. This might mean finding the right job, the right community, or the right social circle. When we find ourselves in an environment that supports our growth and development, we are more likely to succeed.

The second natural law of germination is that a seed must have the right genetics to sprout. Different types of seeds have different requirements for germination. Some seeds, for example, require a period of cold temperatures to break their dormancy. Others may require specific types of soil or light conditions to sprout.

In life, our genetics also play a role in our success. While we can't change our genetic makeup, we can understand our strengths and weaknesses and find ways to work with them. For example, if we know that we have a natural talent for math, we can focus on careers or hobbies that allow us to use that talent to its fullest potential.

The third natural law of germination is that once a seed has sprouted, it must continue to receive the right environment and nutrients to grow into a healthy plant. This means that it needs the right balance of water, nutrients, and light to thrive. If any of these factors are out of balance, the plant may wither and die.

Similarly, in life, success requires ongoing effort and the right balance of resources. This might mean getting enough sleep, eating a healthy diet, and exercising regularly to maintain our physical health. It might also mean cultivating positive relationships and nurturing our mental and emotional well-being.

The fourth natural law of germination is that a plant must adapt to its environment to survive. This means that it must be able to tolerate changes in temperature, moisture, and other environmental factors. Plants that can't adapt to their environment may die out, while those that can adapt are more likely to thrive.

In life, adaptation is also a key component of success. We must be able to adapt to changing circumstances, whether that means learning new skills, taking on new challenges, or adjusting our goals and priorities. Those who are able to adapt and thrive in the face of change are more likely to achieve success in their endeavors.

In conclusion, the natural laws of germination provide us with valuable insights into the principles of success in life. By understanding these laws, we can better understand the factors that contribute to our own success, and take steps to cultivate the right environment, resources, and mindset to help us achieve our goals.

# *Poetic Recap*

*In the cradle of soil, where secrets lie deep, Lies the magic of life, where dreams take their leap. The laws of germination, a tale untold, In nature's embrace, their wonders unfold.*

*Beneath the Earth's blanket, seeds softly rest, In a world of potential, where they are blessed. With moisture and warmth, the spark does ignite, Germination commences, in the softest light.*

*From a tiny seed, a sprout does emerge, Unfurling its leaves, with a determined urge. The laws of germination, in each tender shoot, A promise of life, in pursuit of the root.*

*In the dance of seasons, a symphony unfolds,*

*As germination's story in nature's scroll. From winter's chill to spring's embrace, Seeds awaken with life, at a gentle pace.*
*The laws of germination, a timeless art, A cycle of birth, in which we all take part. From forests to fields, and gardens we tend, Germination's whispers, in every green trend.*

*In patience and faith, we watch them grow, From seedling to tree, in a graceful flow. The laws of germination, a reminder clear, That life's renewal is always near.*

*In the heart of a gardener, hope does reside, With the laws of germination, dreams collide. Nurturing each seedling, with love and care, Witnessing the miracle, as life fills the air.*

*So, let us heed the laws of germination's grace, In nature's rhythm, find our rightful place. A testament to life's enduring sensation, In the laws of germination, a sacred creation.*

## Laws of Attraction

The Law of Attraction is a popular concept that has gained significant attention in recent years, particularly in the personal development and self-help industries. At its core, the Law of Attraction suggests that our thoughts and emotions can have a powerful influence on the events and circumstances that we attract into our lives.

The basic premise of the Law of Attraction is that like attracts like. This means that if we focus our thoughts and emotions on positive things, we are more likely to attract positive experiences and outcomes. Conversely, if we focus on negative thoughts and emotions, we are more likely to attract negative experiences and outcomes.

According to the Law of Attraction, our thoughts and emotions create a vibrational frequency that resonates with similar frequencies in the universe. This means that our internal state has a direct impact on the external world around us, including the people and situations that we attract into our lives.

One of the key principles of the Law of Attraction is the power of visualization. By imagining ourselves already experiencing the outcomes that we desire, we can create a powerful positive vibration that will attract those outcomes into our lives. For example, if we want to attract more abundance into our lives, we might visualize ourselves living in a beautiful home, driving a fancy car, and enjoying financial freedom.

Another important aspect of the Law of Attraction is the importance of gratitude. By expressing gratitude for the things we already have in our lives, we create a positive vibration that attracts more abundance and positivity into our lives. This means that we should focus on being thankful for what we have, rather than dwelling on what we lack.

Critics of the Law of Attraction argue that it is simply a form of magical thinking and that there is no scientific evidence to support its claims. However, proponents of the Law of Attraction argue that it is not a matter of belief, but rather a matter of how we choose to focus our thoughts and emotions. They argue that by shifting our mindset towards positivity and abundance, we can create a more fulfilling and successful life for ourselves.

Regardless of whether or not you believe in the Law of Attraction, there are certainly benefits to focusing on positivity and gratitude in your life. By cultivating a mindset of abundance and positivity, you can create a more joyful and fulfilling life, regardless of the circumstances that you may face.

In conclusion, the Law of Attraction suggests that our thoughts and emotions have a powerful influence on the events and circumstances that we attract into our lives. By focusing on positivity, visualization, and gratitude, we can create a more fulfilling and successful life for ourselves. Whether or not you believe in the Law of Attraction, there is certainly value in cultivating a mindset of abundance and positivity in your life.

## *Poetic Recap*

*In the cosmos' vast expanse, where stars align, Reside the laws of attraction, a force divine. A magnetic pull that draws hearts and dreams near, Invisible threads connecting all we hold dear.*

*Like celestial bodies in the night's grand ballet, Attraction entwines souls in a cosmic display. From galaxies to atoms, in patterns so grand, The laws of attraction shape this wondrous land.*

*In matters of love, where hearts beat as one, Attraction ignites a radiant sun. Two souls converging in a serendipitous way, Guided by the laws, they find their path, they sway.*

*In friendships that form, like magnets they cling,*

*Shared interests and laughter, they're echoing. Attraction is a bridge, a magnetic connection, Uniting kindred spirits in heartfelt affection.*
*In dreams and ambitions, where vision takes flight, Attraction fuels the fire that burns so bright. With intention and focus, we draw our desire, The laws of attraction, our dreams they inspire.*

*Yet, attraction bears a delicate might, For negativity can also take flight. In thoughts and emotions, our energy's key, The laws of attraction reflect what we decree.*

*In the world's grand design, both near and afar, Attraction's the guiding North Star. A reminder to cherish the moments we share, For in attraction's embrace, we find love's affair.*
*So, heed the laws of attraction's sweet call, Let positivity and love be your all. In the cosmic tapestry, where dreams take action, Embrace the power of attraction's magnetic attraction.*

## The Laws of Manifestation

The Laws of Manifestation refer to a set of principles that govern the process of manifesting our desires and intentions into reality. These laws are based on the belief that everything in the universe is made up of energy, and that by aligning our thoughts, beliefs, and actions with this energy, we can attract and create the things we want in life.

There are many different interpretations of the Laws of Manifestation, but some of the most commonly recognized ones are:

1. **The Law of Attraction:** This is perhaps the most well-known law of

manifestation. It states that like attracts like, meaning that the energy we put out into the universe will attract similar energy back to us. In other words, if we focus on positive thoughts and emotions, we will attract positive experiences and opportunities, while negative thoughts and emotions will attract negative experiences and situations.

2. **The Law of Vibration:** This law states that everything in the universe, including our thoughts and emotions, vibrates at a certain frequency. By raising our vibration to a higher level, we can attract and manifest higher-frequency experiences and opportunities. This can be achieved through practices like meditation, gratitude, and positive affirmations.
3. **The Law of Action:** This law emphasizes the importance of taking action towards our goals and desires. While positive

thinking and visualization are important, they are not enough on their own. We must also take inspired action towards our goals in order to manifest them into reality.

4. **The Law of Intention:** This law highlights the importance of setting clear intentions for what we want to manifest. By focusing our attention and energy on our intentions, we can create a powerful force that can help bring our desires into reality.
5. **The Law of Co-creation:** This law recognizes that we are not alone in the process of manifestation. Instead, we are co-creating our reality with the universe and other individuals. By working together in harmony with others and the universe, we can manifest our desires more easily and efficiently.

While these laws are often talked about in the context of material desires like wealth and success, they can also be applied to more spiritual and personal desires like inner peace and happiness. The Laws of Manifestation are not a magical solution or quick fix, but rather a mindset and way of living that can help us align our thoughts, beliefs, and actions with the energy of the universe.

To apply the Laws of Manifestation in our lives, it is important to first identify our desires and intentions. This can be done through self-reflection and introspection, and by setting clear goals and objectives for what we want to achieve. Once we have identified our desires, we can then focus our attention and energy on them through practices like visualization, positive affirmations, and gratitude.

We must also take inspired action towards our goals, and be open to opportunities and experiences that may arise along the way. By staying in a positive and open mindset, we can attract and create the things we want in life.

In conclusion, the Laws of Manifestation are a set of principles that can help us attract and create the things we desire in life. By aligning our thoughts, beliefs, and actions with the energy of the universe, we can manifest our dreams and goals into reality. While it may take time and effort to fully understand and apply these laws in our lives, the rewards of living in alignment with the universe can be truly life-changing.

# *Poetic Recap*

*In the realm of dreams, where desires take flight, Reside the laws of manifestation, pure and bright. A force that shapes reality with unwavering grace, In the cosmic dance, we find our destined place.*

*With thoughts as seeds, we plant our intentions deep, In the fertile soil of the universe, they seep. The laws of manifestation, they silently listen, To the whispers of our hearts, in a world glistening.*

*Through visualization and belief, we ignite the spark, Guiding our dreams from the abyss to embark. In the alchemy of mind, we wield the power, The laws of manifestation, in every waking hour.*

*From dreams to reality, the journey unfolds, As intentions manifest, like stories untold. The laws of manifestation, a bridge to our goal, Transforming thoughts and visions, making them whole.*

*With patience and faith, we trust the design, As the universe aligns, in its grand design. The laws of manifestation, they teach us to wait, For what we conceive, it's never too late.*

*But manifestation's art is more than just wish, It's effort and action, a fulfilling dish. The laws of manifestation, they meet us halfway, Empowering us to create our own day.*

*In this tapestry of life, where dreams take root, The laws of manifestation, they bear the fruit. From vision to reality, we bridge the divide, In the dance of creation, we ride the tide.*

*So, let us honor the laws of manifestation's decree, For they offer the gift of endless possibility. With focus and belief, we shape our destination, In the laws of manifestation, we find our revelation.*

# Laws of Quantum Physics

Quantum physics is a branch of physics that deals with the behavior of matter and energy on an atomic and subatomic scale. It is a relatively new field that emerged in the early 20th century, and it has since revolutionized our understanding of the world. The laws of quantum physics describe the behavior of particles at the atomic level, and they have many applications in modern technology, including computers, cryptography, and medicine.

The fundamental laws of quantum physics are very different from the laws that govern the behavior of larger objects. In classical physics, particles are treated as solid, billiard-ball-like objects that move through space and interact with each other in predictable ways. In contrast, in quantum physics, particles are described by a wave function that gives the probability of finding the particle at any given location. This means that particles can exist in multiple states simultaneously, a phenomenon known as superposition.

One of the most famous laws of quantum physics is the Heisenberg uncertainty principle, which states that the more precisely the position of a particle is known, the less precisely its momentum can be known, and vice versa. This means that it is impossible to know both the position and momentum of a particle with absolute certainty. The uncertainty principle has profound implications for our understanding of the world, as it means that particles are not completely deterministic, and that there is always a degree of uncertainty in our observations.

Another important law of quantum physics is entanglement. Entanglement occurs when two particles become linked in such a way that the state of one particle is dependent on the state of the other, regardless of the distance between them. This means that if one particle is observed and its state is changed, the state of the other particle will also change, instantaneously. This phenomenon has been demonstrated in numerous experiments, and it has many potential applications, including quantum computing and cryptography.

One of the most challenging aspects of quantum physics is the role of observation. In classical physics, observation is seen as a passive act that does not affect the behavior of the object being observed. In contrast, in quantum physics, observation can have a profound impact on the behavior of particles. This is known as the observer effect, and it is related to the concept of wave function collapse. When a particle is observed, its wave function collapses, and it becomes locked into a particular state. This means that observation is not a passive act, but an active intervention that can change the behavior of particles.

The laws of quantum physics have many practical applications in modern technology. One of the most promising is quantum computing, which uses the principles of quantum mechanics to perform calculations that would be impossible for classical computers. Quantum computers are still in the early stages of development, but they have the potential to revolutionize many fields, including cryptography, materials science, and drug discovery.

In conclusion, the laws of quantum physics describe the behavior of particles at the atomic and subatomic level. They are fundamentally different from the laws that govern the behavior of larger objects, and they have many practical applications in modern technology. The laws of quantum physics are still being explored and understood, and they continue to challenge our understanding of the world.

# *Poetic Recap*

*In the realm where atoms dance their cosmic waltz, Lies a world beyond what common sense exalts. Quantum laws, elusive and profound, Unveil the secrets of the universe unbound.*

*In particles so small, they're nearly not, Uncertainty reigns in this quantum plot. Heisenberg's principle, a guiding star, Tells us we can't know both speed and where they are. Superposition, a curious state, A particle exists in a quantum debate. In a mix of all possibilities, it does reside, Until observed, the truth won't be implied.*

*Entanglement, a mystical connection, Defying distance and all convention. Particles entwined, their fates are shared, A cosmic bond, no matter how they're paired.*

*Wave-particle duality, a puzzling scene, Particles act as waves, as if in a dream. They're both a particle and a wave at once, A quantum mystery, a cosmic dance.*

*Einstein's objections, a paradox unfurled, "God does not play dice," he told the world. But quantum dice are rolled with utmost grace, In this strange and wondrous, quantum space. Quantum tunneling, where barriers break, Particles pass through, no matter the stake. A testament to quantum's strange domain, Where reality and fantasy blend, enchain.*

*In quantum's laws, a universe so strange, Our understanding, forever rearrange. A dance of particles, a cosmic rhyme, In this quantum world, we transcend space and time.*

# The Laws of Quantum Mechanics

Quantum mechanics is a branch of physics that describes the behavior of matter and energy at the smallest scales. At this level, classical physics, which governs the behavior of objects in our everyday world, no longer applies. The laws of quantum mechanics, also known as quantum theory, are fundamental principles that describe the behavior of particles at the subatomic level.

One of the key principles of quantum mechanics is the concept of wave-particle duality. This principle suggests that particles, such as electrons and photons, can exhibit both wave-like and particle-like behavior. For example, electrons can behave like particles when they are detected by a detector, but they can also exhibit wave-like behavior when they are not being measured.

Another important principle of quantum mechanics is superposition. This principle suggests that a quantum system can exist in multiple states simultaneously. This means that an electron can exist in multiple positions or energy levels at the same time. However, when the electron is measured or observed, it collapses into a single state.

The uncertainty principle is also a key principle of quantum mechanics. This principle suggests that the position and momentum of a particle cannot be known simultaneously with absolute accuracy. The more accurately the position of a particle is measured, the less accurately its momentum can be known, and vice versa. This principle places a fundamental limit on the precision with which we can measure physical quantities.

Entanglement is another important principle of quantum mechanics. This principle suggests that particles can become entangled, or correlated, in a way that cannot be explained by classical physics. When two particles are entangled, their properties become linked, even when they are separated by vast distances. This principle has been used in experiments to demonstrate the phenomenon of quantum teleportation, where the quantum state of one particle is transferred to another particle without any physical connection between them.

The laws of quantum mechanics also describe the process of quantum tunneling. This phenomenon occurs when a particle is able to pass through a potential barrier that would be impenetrable according to classical physics. Quantum tunneling is important in a wide range of applications, including the behavior of transistors in electronic devices.

The laws of quantum mechanics have been confirmed by numerous experiments, and they have been used to explain a wide range of phenomena in physics, chemistry, and materials science. Quantum mechanics has also played a key role in the development of new technologies, such as quantum computing and quantum cryptography.

Despite its success, quantum mechanics is still not fully understood, and it remains a subject of ongoing research and debate. Some scientists have proposed alternative interpretations of quantum mechanics, such as the many-worlds interpretation or the pilot-wave theory, which seek to explain the strange behavior of particles in a different way.

In conclusion, the laws of quantum mechanics are fundamental principles that describe the behavior of matter and energy at the smallest scales. These laws include wave-particle duality, superposition, the uncertainty principle, entanglement, and quantum tunneling. Quantum mechanics has played a key role in the development of new technologies and has provided a deep understanding of the behavior of particles at the subatomic level. Despite ongoing research and debate, the laws of quantum mechanics are widely accepted as the most accurate description of the behavior of matter and energy at the smallest scales.

## Poetic Recap

*In the quantum realm, where mysteries reside, Lies the dance of particles, where science takes its stride. The laws of quantum mechanics, a cosmic ode, Unveil the universe's secrets on this quantum road.*

*In particles so small, they defy the eye, Quantum laws dictate, they can occupy the sky. Uncertainty's cloak, Heisenberg proclaimed, The more we know of one, the other remains untamed.*

*Superposition's waltz, particles entwined, A paradox where truth and fiction bind. In states of possibility, they do persist, Until observed, their fate remains a twist.*

*Entanglement's embrace, a mystical affair, Particles connected, no matter how far or where. A quantum bond, in the fabric of space, In quantum mechanics, they find their place. Wave-particle duality, a dualistic theme, Particles act as waves, in this quantum dream. A duality that baffles, yet it's scientifically true, Quantum laws unveil a reality quite askew.*

*Einstein's doubt, a paradox he'd revile, "God does not play dice," he'd reconcile. But in quantum dice, a roll with grace, In this strange quantum world, particles embrace.*

*Tunneling through barriers, a quantum delight, Particles pass through, as if taking flight. A testament to quantum's peculiar scheme, Where reality and imagination entwine in the gleam. In quantum mechanics, laws both strange and true, Defying common sense, they dance in view. A universe profound, a cosmic ballet, In the laws of quantum mechanics, we find our way.*

*So, let us marvel at this quantum rhyme, Where particles waltz in a timeless time. In quantum's laws, we find a boundless sea, A universe of wonders, where mysteries are set free.*

# The Laws of Quantum Leaping

Quantum leaping refers to the instantaneous transition of a quantum system from one state to another without passing through any intermediate states. This phenomenon is governed by the laws of quantum mechanics, which provide a mathematical framework for understanding the behavior of quantum systems.

One of the fundamental laws of quantum leaping is the uncertainty principle, which states that the position and momentum of a quantum particle cannot be measured simultaneously with arbitrary precision. This means that the act of measuring one variable affects the other, making it impossible to predict with certainty the future state of the system.

Another important law of quantum leaping is the superposition principle, which states that a quantum system can exist in multiple states simultaneously. This is in contrast to classical systems, where a particle can only exist in one state at a time. The superposition principle allows for the possibility of quantum leaping, as a quantum system can be in two or more states at the same time, making it possible to transition from one state to another without passing through any intermediate states.

The concept of entanglement is also crucial to understanding the laws of quantum leaping. When two quantum systems interact, they can become entangled, meaning that the state of one system is dependent on the state of the other. This allows for the possibility of quantum leaping between entangled systems, as a change in the state of one system can instantaneously affect the state of the other.

The laws of quantum leaping have important implications for a wide range of fields, including quantum computing, quantum cryptography, and quantum teleportation. In quantum computing, the ability to perform operations on multiple states simultaneously allows for the development of algorithms that are much more efficient than classical algorithms. In quantum cryptography, the laws of quantum leaping are used to create secure communication channels that are resistant to eavesdropping. In quantum teleportation, entanglement is used to transfer the state of one quantum system to another without physically moving the system itself.

While the laws of quantum leaping have been extensively studied and validated through experiments, they also raise many philosophical questions about the nature of reality. For example, the superposition principle implies that a particle can exist in multiple states simultaneously, but when a measurement is made, the particle collapses into a single state. This has led some physicists to propose the existence of a "many-worlds" interpretation of quantum mechanics, where every possible outcome of a quantum event exists in a separate parallel universe.

In conclusion, the laws of quantum leaping are a fundamental part of quantum mechanics, governing the behavior of quantum systems at the smallest scales. These laws have important practical applications in fields such as quantum computing and cryptography, but also raise profound questions about the nature of reality and the structure of the universe. As our understanding of quantum mechanics continues to evolve, it is likely that new insights into the laws of quantum leaping will emerge, leading to new advances in technology and a deeper understanding of the world around us.

# *Poetic Recap*

*In the quantum tapestry, a phenomenon profound, Lies the enigma of leaping, where mysteries are unbound. The laws of quantum leaping, a cosmic ballet, Unveil the universe's secrets in an intricate display.*

*In the realm of the small, where particles reside, Quantum leaps occur as they swiftly glide. From one energy state to another they soar, The laws of quantum leaping, their essence we explore.*

*Electrons in orbit, a dance so divine, Leap to new shells, in a quantum design. A discontinuous journey, through energy's stair, The laws of quantum leaping, they take us there.*

*In the heart of the atom, a nucleus's hold, Protons and neutrons, in a quantum threshold. They, too, can leap, in a nuclear shift, The laws of quantum leaping, their motion swift.*

*In the cosmos' vastness, stars take their cue, Quantum leaps of light, in the night's dark hue. From nuclear fusion to the twinkle in the sky, The laws of quantum leaping, their brilliance is nigh.*

*Yet quantum leaping's art is not confined, To particles and photons, it's intertwined. In human consciousness, thoughts can leap and soar, The laws of quantum leaping, we explore more.*

*From a state of despair to one of elation, Quantum leaps in emotions, a soul's salvation. In the realms of the mind, where dreams ignite, The laws of quantum leaping, in our inner light.*

*In the grand design of life, we find our place, In quantum leaping's rhythm, we embrace. A testament to possibilities untold, The laws of quantum leaping, in them, we unfold.*

*So, let us marvel at this quantum rhyme, Where leaps of existence transcend space and time. In quantum's laws, a dance forever deep, A universe of wonders, where quantum leaps we keep.*

# TUNING TO A HIGHER FREQUENCY

Tuning to higher frequencies is a concept that has gained a lot of attention in recent times, especially in the field of spiritual and metaphysical practices. It refers to the process of raising one's vibration or energy frequency to a higher level, which is believed to lead to greater clarity, vitality, and well-being. In this article, we will explore what tuning to higher frequencies means, why it is important, and some effective ways to achieve it.

Firstly, it is important to understand what we mean by frequency. Everything in the universe, including our bodies and thoughts, vibrates at a certain frequency. This frequency can be measured in Hertz (Hz), and it determines the quality of our experiences. Lower frequencies are associated with negative emotions like fear, anger, and sadness, while higher frequencies are associated with positive emotions like love, joy, and peace.

Tuning to higher frequencies means consciously choosing to shift our energy from a lower to a higher frequency. This can be done through a variety of practices, including meditation, yoga, breathwork, visualization, and energy healing. By raising our vibration, we can become more aligned with our true selves, connect more deeply with others, and manifest the life we desire.

So why is tuning to higher frequencies important? The answer lies in the law of attraction, which states that like attracts like. When we are vibrating at a high frequency, we attract positive experiences, people, and circumstances into our lives. On the other hand, when we are vibrating at a low frequency, we attract negative experiences, people, and circumstances. Therefore, by tuning to higher frequencies, we can create a life that is filled with abundance, joy, and love.

One effective way to tune to higher frequencies is through meditation. Meditation allows us to quiet our minds, focus on the present moment, and connect with our inner selves. This, in turn, raises our vibration and helps us to access higher states of consciousness. There are many different types of meditation, including mindfulness meditation, loving-kindness meditation, and transcendental meditation. The key is to find a style that resonates with you and commit to a regular practice.

Another way to tune to higher frequencies is through yoga. Yoga is an ancient practice that combines physical postures with breathwork and meditation. It helps to balance our energy centers, or chakras, and release any blockages that may be keeping us stuck in lower frequencies. Yoga also strengthens our physical bodies, improves our flexibility and mobility, and promotes overall health and well-being.

Breathwork is another powerful tool for tuning to higher frequencies. By consciously controlling our breath, we can activate our parasympathetic nervous system, which helps us to relax and reduce stress. This, in turn, raises our vibration and allows us to access higher states of consciousness. There are many different types of breathwork, including pranayama, holotropic breathing, and rebirthing. The key is to find a style that works for you and practice it regularly.

Visualization is another effective way to tune to higher frequencies. By visualizing positive outcomes and feeling the emotions associated with them, we can attract those experiences into our lives. Visualization can be done through guided meditations, vision boards, or simply by closing your eyes and imagining your ideal life. The key is to make your visualizations as vivid and detailed as possible and to practice them consistently.

Finally, energy healing is a powerful way to tune to higher frequencies. Energy healing modalities like Reiki, acupuncture, and sound healing work by clearing blockages in our energy field and balancing our chakras. This, in turn, raises our vibration and allows us to access higher states of consciousness. Energy healing can be done by a trained practitioner or by yourself, using techniques like self-Reiki or acupress.

# *Poetic Recap*

*In the symphony of existence, a subtle refrain, A call to ascend, to a higher plane. Tuning to a higher frequency, a cosmic art, A journey of the soul, a transcendent start.*

*In the realm of vibrations, where energy resides, Higher frequencies beckon, like ocean tides. They ripple through the soul, like a gentle breeze, Awakening dormant senses, with a sense of ease.*

*In stillness, we find it, a serene vibration, A resonance with truth, a divine sensation. Tuning to a higher frequency, we elevate, From the mundane to the profound, we navigate.*

*In thoughts and intentions, we set our course,*

*To align with the cosmos, to gather its force. Higher frequencies bring clarity and grace, A sacred path to follow, in life's cosmic space.*

*From fear to love, from ego to soul, Higher frequencies transform, making us whole. The ego's grip loosens, as the heart takes flight, In the radiant glow of a higher light.*

*In meditation's embrace, we find the way, To tune into frequencies that gently sway. The universe's wisdom, in silence we receive, As we attune to a higher frequency, we believe.*

*In the dance of connection, we join the song, A harmonious chorus where we all belong. Tuning to a higher frequency, hand in hand, We co-create a world where love does expand. So, let us heed the call, in unity, To raise our vibrations, to be truly free. Tuning to a higher frequency, we take our cue, In this cosmic journey, where dreams come true.*

*In the grand symphony of life, we play our part, Tuning to a higher frequency, with an open heart. A celestial melody, in the vast cosmic sea, Tuning to a higher frequency, we find our destiny.*

# Nikola Tesla's 3,6,9 Number Sequence

The Nikola Tesla 3, 6, 9 number sequence is a mysterious and intriguing concept that has fascinated people for many years. Tesla was a brilliant inventor, scientist, and engineer who made significant contributions to the fields of electricity, magnetism, and electromagnetism. He was also known for his unusual ideas and beliefs, and the 3, 6, 9 sequence is one of the most intriguing.

The basic idea behind the 3, 6, 9 sequence is that everything in the universe can be explained using these three numbers. Tesla believed that the key to unlocking the secrets of the universe lay in understanding the significance of these numbers and how they relate to one another.

According to Tesla, the number 3 is the key to understanding the universe because it is the basis for all physical phenomena. He believed that everything in the universe could be explained in terms of three basic elements: energy, vibration, and frequency. He also believed that the number 3 was significant because it represented the Trinity in Christianity and was a fundamental concept in many other religions and cultures.

The number 6, according to Tesla, was significant because it represented balance and harmony in the universe. He believed that the number 6 was the key to understanding the relationships between different elements in the universe and that it was the basis for all mathematical calculations.

Finally, Tesla believed that the number 9 was the most important of all. He believed that the number 9 was the key to unlocking the secrets of the universe and that it represented the ultimate expression of all physical phenomena. According to Tesla, the number 9 was the most powerful number in the universe because it was the highest single-digit number and contained within it all other numbers.

Many people have tried to decipher the meaning behind Tesla's 3, 6, 9 sequence, but it remains a mystery to this day. Some people believe that the sequence is a code that Tesla used to communicate his ideas to others, while others believe that it was simply a personal obsession of his.

Regardless of its true meaning, the 3, 6, 9 sequence has captured the imagination of people around the world and has inspired countless artists, musicians, and writers. Many people believe that the sequence represents a fundamental truth about the universe, and that understanding its significance is key to unlocking the secrets of the cosmos.

One interesting application of the 3, 6, 9 sequence is in the field of music. Many musicians believe that the sequence represents a fundamental truth about the relationships between different musical notes and that understanding this relationship is key to creating beautiful and harmonious music.

Overall, the Nikola Tesla 3, 6, 9 number sequence remains a mystery to this day, but its significance and importance cannot be denied. Whether it is a code, a personal obsession, or a fundamental truth about the universe, the sequence continues to inspire and captivate people around the world.

# *Poetic Recap*

*In the mind of Tesla, a genius's decree, Lies the enigma of numbers, a mystery key. Three, six, and nine, in a sequence divine, Unveil the secrets of the universe's design.*

*Tesla, the wizard of electricity's might, Sought patterns in numbers, in the day and the night. In the triad of numbers, a truth he did see, Three, six, and nine, they held the master key.*

*In cycles and rhythms, nature's grand score, Three-fold symmetry, at its very core. From galaxies to flowers, in beauty and grace, The numbers resonate, in every place.*

*Three, the beginning, a creative spark, Six, the harmony, where the world finds its mark. But Tesla, he knew, in the quietest line, Nine held the secret, in its form so divine.*

*In the sum of all numbers, a pattern did gleam, Three plus six plus nine, a recurring theme. Infinite energy, Tesla foresaw, In the numbers' dance, he found no flaw.*

*In resonance's power, he sought to employ, Tesla's inventions, a source of great joy. Three, six, and nine, in frequencies high, They held the future, in the blink of an eye.*

*In Tesla's world, where science did soar, Three, six, and nine, they opened the door. To a world of possibilities, where energy's free, In the number sequence, Tesla's legacy.*

*In the grand scheme of life, a cosmic rhyme, Three, six, and nine, through the sands of time.*

*In the laws of the universe, they forever shine,*
*Nikola Tesla's numbers, a gift so fine.*

*So, let us remember the wisdom he shared, In the numbers' sequence, where Tesla dared. To unlock the mysteries, in the grandest design, Three, six, and nine, they forever align.*

# What is The Reticular Activator?

The Reticular Activator (RA) is a network of nerve cells located in the brainstem, responsible for regulating various functions such as sleep, arousal, attention, and alertness. It is often referred to as the Reticular Activating System or RAS.

The RA is a complex network of neurons that receives input from various sensory systems, such as vision, hearing, touch, and smell. It also receives input from higher cognitive functions, such as memory, emotion, and motivation. The RA acts as a filter, screening out irrelevant sensory input and focusing attention on important stimuli. This filtering mechanism helps to prevent sensory overload and allows individuals to selectively attend to stimuli that are relevant to their current goals.

One of the most important functions of the RA is its role in regulating sleep and wakefulness.

The RA is responsible for maintaining a state of wakefulness and alertness during the day, and for promoting sleep at night. The RA achieves this by releasing a neurotransmitter called norepinephrine, which is involved in arousal and alertness. Norepinephrine acts on various parts of the brain, including the thalamus and cortex, to enhance neuronal activity and promote wakefulness.

In addition to its role in sleep and wakefulness, the RA is also involved in other cognitive processes such as attention and memory. The RA is responsible for filtering out irrelevant sensory information and focusing attention on important stimuli. This filtering mechanism is crucial for allowing individuals to selectively attend to stimuli that are relevant to their current goals. The RA also plays a role in memory consolidation, the process by which memories are transferred from short-term to long-term storage.

The RA is also involved in regulating emotional responses. It receives input from the limbic system, which is responsible for processing emotions, and can modulate emotional responses through its influence on other brain regions. For example, the RA can activate the amygdala, a brain region involved in fear and anxiety, to produce a fight or flight response.

Finally, the RA has been implicated in a number of neurological disorders. Dysfunction of the RA has been linked to attention deficit hyperactivity disorder (ADHD), depression, and other psychiatric conditions. In ADHD, for example, the RA may be less active, leading to difficulties with attention and hyperactivity. In depression, the RA may be overactive, leading to a state of chronic arousal and insomnia.

In conclusion, the Reticular Activator is a complex network of neurons located in the brainstem, responsible for regulating various functions such as sleep, arousal, attention, and alertness. Its filtering mechanism helps to prevent sensory overload and allows individuals to selectively attend to stimuli that are relevant to their current goals. The RA also plays a role in memory consolidation, emotional responses, and has been implicated in various neurological disorders. Understanding the function of the RA is crucial for understanding normal cognitive processes and for developing treatments for neurological disorders.

And in other words… as it relates to the law of attraction…

The reticular activating system (RAS) is

a fascinating neural network located within the brainstem that plays a crucial role in regulating arousal, attention, and awareness. While the concept of the RAS is well-established in neuroscience, its connection to the law of attraction is often described in more metaphysical terms.

In the context of the law of attraction, proponents suggest that the RAS can act as a filter for the vast amount of sensory information bombarding our senses at any given moment. According to this theory, the RAS filters and prioritizes information that aligns with our thoughts, beliefs, and desires, effectively influencing what we perceive and focus on in our reality.

Proponents of the law of attraction propose that by consciously directing our thoughts and intentions towards our goals, we can activate the RAS to seek out relevant opportunities and experiences in our environment. This is believed to create a sort of positive feedback loop: as we focus on specific goals, the RAS heightens our awareness of related circumstances, coincidences, and resources that might otherwise go unnoticed.

Critics, however, argue that the connection between the RAS and the law of attraction remains largely speculative and lacks empirical evidence. While the RAS undeniably plays a role in information processing and filtering, attributing mystical or universal powers to it can be viewed as an oversimplification of its complex functions.

In sum, the reticular activating system is an integral component of our brain's architecture, influencing our wakefulness and perception. In the realm of the law of attraction, it is posited that by harnessing the power of the RAS through focused intention and positive thinking, individuals can potentially enhance their ability to manifest their desires. Whether viewed through a neurological or metaphysical lens, the interplay between the reticular activating system and the law of attraction remains a subject of ongoing exploration and debate.

## *Poetic Recap*

*In the depths of consciousness, a subtle guide, Resides the reticular activator, by our side. A filter for our senses, a masterful gate, Unveiling the power to navigate our fate.*

*Within the labyrinth of thoughts, it takes its place, The reticular activator, with quiet grace. A neural network, a sentinel's role, To focus our attention on a chosen goal.*

*In the cacophony of life's bustling stream, The reticular activator fulfills its dream. It screens the noise, the chaos, and the crowd, Directing our awareness, like a compass proud.*

*With intention's spark, it comes alive, Guiding our perception, helping us to thrive. The reticular activator, a beacon's light, Illuminates our path through day and night.*
*In dreams and aspirations, it plays its part, The reticular activator fuels the heart. With clarity and purpose, it sets the stage, To manifest desires, at any life's age.*

*Yet in this digital age, with stimuli abound, The reticular activator can sometimes be drowned. Overwhelmed by input, in a world so fast, We must cherish its gift, as we journey past.*

*In the grand design of mind and brain, The reticular activator helps us gain. A focus on what truly matters most, In its silent guidance, we find our utmost.*

*So, let us honor this neural guide, The reticular activator, always by our side. In conscious intention, we discover the key, To harness its power and set ourselves free.*

*In the intricate tapestry of life's grand parade, The reticular activator, our goals it will aid. With clarity and vision, we set our sail, On the seas of purpose, where our dreams prevail.*

# ASK THE UNIVERSE…

## *Poetic Pre-Recap*

*In the realm of dreams, where stars ignite, Lies the magic of asking the universe, so bright. With whispers of hope and hearts open wide, We seek the cosmos' secrets, on this cosmic ride.*

*In the silence of night, beneath moon's soft glow, We send out our wishes, like seeds we sow. The magic of asking, a humble plea, To the vast universe, on bended knee.*

*With questions and desires, we cast our spell, Asking the universe, our stories to tell. In the language of dreams, we dare to inquire, Unlocking the cosmic vaults, our spirits aspire.*

*In nature's embrace, we find our muse, Asking the universe, we'll never lose. For in every leaf's rustle, and every wave's crest, The universe responds, at its very best.*
*With gratitude's grace, we count our stars, Asking the universe, from afar. In each breath we take, and each step we trod, The magic of asking, connects us to God.*

*In the tapestry of life, where dreams unfold, Asking the universe, with intentions bold. The cosmos listens, in silence it waits, To grant our wishes, to unlock the gates.*

*But in this sacred dance, there's more to find, The magic of asking is heart, soul, and mind. For with action and effort, we shape our fate, In partnership with the universe, we co-create. So, let us embrace this enchanting art, The magic of asking, where dreams take part. With faith and conviction, let your wishes unfurl,*

*And watch as the universe, in wonder, unfurls.*

## What is Access Consciousness?

Access Consciousness is a personal development program founded by Gary Douglas and Dr. Dain Heer in the late 1990s. It is a set of tools and techniques designed to help individuals expand their consciousness and transform their lives. The Access Consciousness program has become increasingly popular over the years, with thousands of people around the world attending workshops and using its tools.

At the core of Access Consciousness is the concept that individuals have the capacity to be aware of and change anything in their lives. This is based on the premise that we are all infinite beings, with infinite potential and possibilities.

However, our access to this infinite potential is limited by our beliefs, thoughts, and emotions. Access Consciousness provides a set of tools and techniques that allow individuals to release limiting beliefs and emotions and expand their awareness. These tools include verbal processes, energy work, and body work.

One of the key tools of Access Consciousness is the Access Bars, a technique in which the practitioner lightly touches specific points on the head to release stored energy and limiting beliefs. The Access Bars can help to clear the mind, reduce stress and anxiety, improve sleep, and increase overall wellbeing.

Another tool of Access Consciousness is the verbal processes, which are designed to help individuals become aware of and release limiting beliefs and emotions. These processes involve asking questions, such as "What else is possible?" or "What would it take to change this?" The idea behind these questions is to open up possibilities and encourage individuals to let go of limiting beliefs.

Access Consciousness also includes body work techniques, such as Access Facelift and Access Body Processes. These techniques are designed to release tension and trauma from the body and promote healing.

One of the key principles of Access Consciousness is the idea of total allowance. This means allowing everything in your life, including your thoughts, emotions, and experiences, without judgment or resistance. The idea is that when you allow everything in your life, you can more easily release limiting beliefs and emotions and expand your awareness.

Access Consciousness has been criticized by some for its unconventional approach and lack of scientific evidence. However, many people who have used the program report significant improvements in their lives, including increased happiness, better relationships, improved health, and greater success.

In conclusion, Access Consciousness is a personal development program designed to help individuals expand their awareness and transform their lives. Its tools and techniques, such as the Access Bars, verbal processes, and body work, are designed to release limiting beliefs and emotions and promote healing.

The program is based on the principle of total allowance, which encourages individuals to allow everything in their lives without judgment or resistance. While some may criticize Access Consciousness for its unconventional approach, many people have reported significant improvements in their lives as a result of using its tools and techniques.

# 18 QUESTIONS

(18 powerful abundance and manifesting questions as put forth by the principles of access consciousness, that stimulate the mind to orient itself to receive total material, spiritual, and emotional abundance)

1. What would it take for me to be open to receiving abundance in all areas of my life?
2. What beliefs or attitudes am I holding onto that are blocking abundance from flowing to me?
3. How can I expand my capacity to receive more abundance in my life?
4. What actions can I take today to align with the energy of abundance?
5. What would it feel like to be truly

abundant in all areas of my life?

6. What limiting beliefs do I need to let go of to manifest abundance effortlessly?
7. What does abundance mean to me, and how can I align my thoughts and actions with that definition?
8. What changes can I make in my daily routine to invite abundance into my life?
9. What would my life look like if I allowed myself to fully receive all the abundance that the universe has to offer?
10. How can I shift my focus from lack to abundance in my daily thoughts and actions?
11. What positive affirmations can I use to shift my mindset to one of abundance?
12. How can I release any fears or doubts that are preventing me from manifesting abundance?
13. What actions can I take to increase my

feelings of self-worth and deservingness of abundance?

14. What opportunities for abundance am I currently overlooking or dismissing?
15. How can I use my unique skills and talents to create abundance in my life and the world around me?
16. What resources or support do I need to manifest abundance in my life?
17. What lessons can I learn from past experiences of abundance and lack to guide me towards a more abundant future?
18. What can I do right now to express gratitude for the abundance that is already present in my life?

## *Poetic Recap*

*In the realms of awareness, where wisdom abounds, Lies the treasure of consciousness, a profound sound. Accessing the depths of our innermost self, We embark on a journey, in search of life's wealth.*

*With open hearts and curious minds in tow, Access Consciousness invites us to know. The layers of being, the stories we hold, In its embrace, our truths will unfold.*

*From limiting beliefs to patterns that bind, Access Consciousness frees the confines of the mind. A gentle release of what no longer serves, In its loving guidance, our spirit preserves.*

*In the theater of thought, where stories reside, Access Consciousness shows us a path to decide. To rewrite the scripts, to choose our own way, In the radiant light of a brand-new day.*

*With awareness as a lantern, we venture within, Accessing the wisdom, where healing begins. From judgments to forgiveness, we break the chain, In the playground of consciousness, we find no disdain.*

*In the dance of energies, we learn to discern, Access Consciousness, a sacred return. To our authentic self, to the love that's inside, In its gentle embrace, our soul does confide.*

*So, let us embark on this quest profound, Access Consciousness, where treasures are found. In the exploration of self, in the depths we roam, In its radiant embrace, we find our true home. A journey of knowing, a pathway to grace,*

*Access Consciousness, in its boundless embrace.*

*With each step we take, with each truth we confess, In the world of consciousness, we find endless progress.*

# Exploring Nikola Tesla's 3,6,9 Sequence

The Nikola Tesla 3, 6, 9 number sequence has gained a significant amount of attention and fascination in recent years, particularly among those interested in spirituality, numerology, and alternative sciences. The sequence is often associated with mystical and esoteric meanings, and many people believe that understanding the sequence's underlying pattern can unlock secrets of the universe. One of the key aspects of this sequence is finding the common root numbers that tie the sequence together.

The sequence itself is fairly straightforward: starting with the number three, each subsequent number is twice the previous number. So, the sequence goes: 3, 6, 12, 24, 48, 96, and so on. However, what makes this sequence so intriguing is the fact that when you add up the digits of each number in the sequence and reduce them to a single digit, they all result in either 3, 6, or 9.

For example, the digit sum of 3 is 3, the digit sum of 6 is 6, and the digit sum of 12 is 1+2=3. Similarly, the digit sum of 24 is 2+4=6, and the digit sum of 48 is 4+8=12, which reduces to 1+2=3. This pattern continues with each subsequent number in the sequence, all the way up to infinity.

So, what is the significance of these numbers? According to some interpretations, the numbers 3, 6, and 9 are the key to understanding the universe's underlying structure. They are said to represent the fundamental forces of creation, preservation, and destruction, respectively. In this way, the sequence is seen as a metaphor for the cycle of birth, life, and death.

Furthermore, some believe that these numbers hold special significance because of their mathematical properties. For example, 3 is the only number that, when multiplied by itself, produces a number that ends in 9. 6 is the product of 2 and 3, which are both key numbers in many spiritual and religious traditions. And 9 is the highest single-digit number, representing completion and wholeness.

But what about the common root numbers that tie the sequence together? How can we find them, and what do they mean? To understand this, we need to look at the concept of numerology, which is the study of the spiritual significance of numbers.

In numerology, the digits of a number are believed to hold symbolic meaning. For example, the number 1 represents individuality and leadership, while the number 2 represents balance and harmony. When we add up the digits of a number and reduce them to a single digit, we can gain insight into the number's underlying energy or vibration.

So, when we add up the digits of the numbers in the Tesla sequence and reduce them to a single digit, we get:

- 3: 3
- 6: 6
- 12: 1+2=3
- 24: 2+4=6
- 48: 4+8=12, 1+2=3
- 96: 9+6=15, 1+5=6

As we can see, the common root numbers in the Tesla sequence are 3, 6, and 9. These numbers are said to represent the highest levels of spiritual consciousness and divine understanding. They are also associated with creativity, intuition, and manifestation.

In conclusion, the Nikola Tesla 3, 6, 9 number sequence is a fascinating and mysterious phenomenon that has captured the imagination of many people. While the sequence itself is simple, its connection to the numbers 3, 6, and 9 has led to a wide range of interpretations and speculations about its significance. The common root numbers of 3, 6, and 9 have particular importance in numerology and spiritual traditions, and understanding their connection to the Tesla sequence may provide deeper insight into the nature of reality.

One interpretation of the significance of the Tesla sequence is that it represents a fundamental pattern of creation and manifestation. The sequence begins with the number 3, which is associated with the energy of creativity and self-expression. The number 6, which follows 3, represents balance and harmony, and is said to bring stability to creative energy. Finally, the number 9 represents completion and spiritual fulfillment, indicating that the cycle of creation and manifestation has come to its natural end.

Another interpretation of the significance of the Tesla sequence is that it represents a form of sacred geometry, a concept that has been explored in various spiritual traditions for centuries. Sacred geometry is the study of the underlying patterns and structures of the universe, and is believed to hold deep spiritual significance. The Tesla sequence, with its repetitive pattern and connection to the numbers 3, 6, and 9, may be seen as an example of sacred geometry in action.

In addition to its spiritual significance, the Tesla sequence has also been explored for its potential practical applications. Some researchers have suggested that the sequence may hold the key to unlocking new forms of energy, or to developing more efficient ways of harnessing existing energy sources. Tesla himself was known for his pioneering work in the field of electrical engineering, and it is possible that the sequence he identified may have practical implications in this field as well.

Despite the many interpretations and speculations about the significance of the Tesla sequence, its true nature remains elusive. Some see it as a powerful tool for unlocking the secrets of the universe, while others view it as a fascinating but ultimately meaningless curiosity. Whatever one's perspective on the sequence, however, it is clear that it has captured the imagination of many people around the world, and has become a symbol of the human quest for knowledge and understanding.

## Revisiting The Law of Mentalism

The law of mentalism is a principle that asserts that the universe is mental in nature. According to this law, the entire universe is made up of consciousness or mind, and all things that exist are created by this consciousness. The law of mentalism is a foundational principle of the Hermetic philosophy, which is a set of spiritual and philosophical teachings that originated in ancient Egypt and Greece.

The Hermetic philosophy is based on the teachings of Hermes Trismegistus, an ancient Egyptian sage who was believed to possess knowledge of both the physical and spiritual realms. The philosophy teaches that the universe is governed by seven universal principles, one of which is the law of mentalism. This principle states that the universe is mental and that everything in existence is a product of the mind.

The law of mentalism is a complex principle that requires a deep understanding of consciousness and the nature of reality. It is based on the idea that the mind is the creator of all things and that everything we experience is a product of our own perception. This means that the world we experience is a reflection of our own thoughts and beliefs, and that we have the power to change our reality by changing our thoughts.

The law of mentalism has profound implications for our understanding of the world and our place in it. It suggests that we have the power to shape our own reality and that our thoughts and beliefs can have a profound impact on our lives. It also suggests that the universe is interconnected and that everything is part of a larger whole.

The law of mentalism is not a new concept, and it has been explored by many spiritual and philosophical traditions throughout history. For example, the Buddhist tradition teaches that reality is created by the mind, and that our perception of the world is a product of our own consciousness. Similarly, the Hindu tradition teaches that the universe is a manifestation of the divine consciousness, and that all things are ultimately one.

Despite its ancient roots, the law of mentalism has gained renewed interest in recent years due to the growing popularity of the New Age movement and the rise of mindfulness practices. Many people are now exploring the power of the mind and the role it plays in shaping our reality. They are using meditation, visualization, and other techniques to harness the power of the mind and create the life they desire.

In conclusion, the law of mentalism is a powerful principle that has the potential to transform our understanding of the world and our place in it.

It suggests that the universe is mental in nature and that everything we experience is a product of our own perception. By understanding this principle, we can harness the power of the mind and create the life we desire.

## *Poetic Recap*

*In the boundless expanse of the mind's terrain, Lies the profound law of mentalism, a timeless refrain. As above, so below, as within, so without, In the realm of thought, we dance and doubt.*

*Mentalism teaches the power of thought's sway, In the grand symphony of night and day. Thoughts are the architects of our reality's scheme, In the tapestry of existence, they form and gleam.*

*In the silence of minds, where secrets reside, Mentalism unveils the world we decide. Our thoughts are the brushstrokes, our canvas is clear, In the masterpiece of life, we create without fear.*

*As the universe's mirror, our minds reflect, The law of mentalism, its truth we detect. With intention and focus, our dreams take the stage, In the theater of thoughts, they dance in a cage. In the cycles of life, the seasons unfold, Mentalism's story, in patterns untold. From the seed to the tree, in its majesty's span, Thoughts give birth to creation, in the cosmic plan.*

*But mentalism's power is not without care, For thoughts can bring darkness, or love's tender share. In the laws of the mind, we must be aware, The law of mentalism, a force so rare. In the grand cosmic dance, we're the choreographers true, Mentalism's teachings, they guide what we do. With clarity and wisdom, we craft our life's rhyme, In the realm of thought, through the fabric of time.*

*So, let us honor the law, with minds awake,*

*Mentalism's power, for our dreams' sake. With thoughts that are noble, and intentions pure, In the world of the mind, our destiny's secure.*

*In the law of mentalism, we hold the key, To unlock the potential, in you and me. As co-creators of existence, we find our bliss, In the realm of the mind, in the thoughts we kiss.*

# What is Reality Transurfing?

Transurfing is a theory that was developed by the Russian quantum physicist Vadim Zeland. It is a philosophy that explores the concept of reality creation and the idea that we can shift our reality by changing our thoughts, emotions, and actions. Transurfing is based on the principles of quantum physics and the understanding that everything in the universe is connected through energy fields.

The basic principle of Transurfing is that we all have a natural ability to create our own reality. However, our beliefs, emotions, and behaviors can prevent us from manifesting our desires. Transurfing teaches us that by understanding and controlling these factors, we can shape our reality in the way that we desire.

According to Transurfing, there are two main levels of reality: the material and the wave.

The material level is the physical reality that we experience with our senses. The wave level, on the other hand, is the level of energy and vibration that exists beyond the physical realm. According to Transurfing, the wave level is where all possibilities exist, and we can access this level to manifest our desires.

One of the core concepts of Transurfing is the idea of the "space of variations." This refers to the infinite possibilities that exist in the wave level. According to Transurfing, every decision we make creates a ripple effect in the space of variations. By aligning our thoughts, emotions, and actions with our desires, we can shift our reality to align with our intentions.

Transurfing also emphasizes the importance of the "balance of power." This refers to the idea that our thoughts, emotions, and actions must be in alignment with our desires for us to manifest them. If we have conflicting beliefs or emotions, we create resistance that prevents us from achieving our goals.

Another key concept of Transurfing is the idea of "pendulums." Pendulums are energy fields that are created by groups of people who share similar beliefs, values, or interests. These pendulums can influence our thoughts, emotions, and behaviors, and can prevent us from manifesting our desires. Transurfing teaches us to be aware of these pendulums and to detach from them to avoid being influenced by them.

Transurfing also emphasizes the importance of detachment. According to Transurfing, we should focus on our desires, but not become attached to them. When we become too attached to our desires, we create resistance and prevent them from manifesting. Instead, we should focus on the process of creating our reality and trust that our desires will manifest when the time is right.

In conclusion, Transurfing is a powerful philosophy that offers a new perspective on reality creation. It teaches us that we have the power to shape our reality by controlling our thoughts, emotions, and actions. By understanding the principles of Transurfing and applying them in our lives, we can achieve our goals and create the life that we desire.

Transurfing offers a unique perspective on reality creation that has gained popularity in recent years. It offers practical tools for manifesting our desires and shifting our reality in a positive direction. In this section, we will explore some of the key concepts of Transurfing in more detail.

## The Space of Variations

One of the most important concepts in Transurfing is the "space of variations." According to Transurfing, the space of variations is the realm of all possibilities. It is where all potential realities exist, and we can access this realm to manifest our desires.

To access the space of variations, we must align our thoughts, emotions, and actions with our desires. This means focusing our attention on what we want, rather than what we don't want. We must also cultivate positive emotions and beliefs that support our desires.

# The Balance of Power

Another important concept in Transurfing is the "balance of power." According to Transurfing, the balance of power is the state of alignment between our thoughts, emotions, and actions. When we are in balance, we are able to manifest our desires with ease.

However, when we have conflicting thoughts, emotions, or actions, we create resistance that prevents us from achieving our goals. This is why it is important to cultivate a state of balance in our lives. We must align our thoughts, emotions, and actions with our desires to create the reality we want.

## Pendulums

Another key concept in Transurfing is the idea of "pendulums." Pendulums are energy fields that are created by groups of people who share similar beliefs, values, or interests. These pendulums can influence our thoughts, emotions, and behaviors, and can prevent us from manifesting our desires.

Pendulums can be positive or negative. Positive pendulums are those that support our desires and goals, while negative pendulums create resistance and obstacles. To manifest our desires, we must detach from negative pendulums and focus on positive ones.

## Detachment

Another important concept in Transurfing is the idea of detachment. According to Transurfing, we should focus on our desires, but not become attached to them. When we become too attached to our desires, we create resistance and prevent them from manifesting.

Detachment means trusting the process of reality creation and focusing on the present moment. We must cultivate a sense of inner peace and calmness, rather than feeling anxious or desperate for our desires to manifest. This allows us to detach from the outcome and trust that our desires will manifest in the right way and at the right time.

# Reality Transurfing Techniques

Transurfing offers a range of techniques and exercises for shifting our reality and manifesting our desires. Some of the most popular techniques include:

- **Reality Transurfing meditation:** This is a powerful meditation technique that involves accessing the space of variations and visualizing our desires as already manifest. This helps to align our thoughts, emotions, and actions with our desires, creating a state of balance and harmony.
- **Pendulum Detachment:** This technique involves becoming aware of negative pendulums that are influencing our thoughts, emotions, and behaviors. Once

we are aware of these pendulums, we can detach from them and focus on positive ones that support our desires.

- **The Intention Mantra:** This is a simple mantra that involves repeating our intentions to ourselves in a positive and empowering way. By focusing our attention on our desires and speaking them into existence, we create a powerful energy that supports manifestation.
- **The Mirror Technique:** This technique involves looking into a mirror and visualizing ourselves as already having achieved our desires. This helps to cultivate positive emotions and beliefs that support our desires, creating a state of balance and harmony.

## To summarize:

Reality Transurfing is a spiritual and philosophical theory created by Russian quantum physicist Vadim Zeland. It is based on the premise that there are infinite parallel universes, and our choices and intentions allow us to access and navigate through these universes.

According to Reality Transurfing, we are constantly creating our reality by the thoughts and emotions we focus on. Our thoughts and emotions create an energy that attracts similar energy from the universe, which in turn manifests into our reality. Therefore, by shifting our thoughts and emotions, we can alter the reality we experience.

Reality Transurfing suggests that there are five main principles that govern the laws of the universe, which are intention, balance, alternatives, variants, and importance. Intention is the driving force that determines our reality, and balance refers to the equal exchange of energy between our intentions and the universe. Alternatives and variants refer to the many possible realities we can access, and importance is the degree of significance we give to our desires.

One of the key principles of Reality Transurfing is the concept of pendulums. Pendulums are energy fields created by collective thoughts and emotions that can influence our reality. They can be positive or negative and can have a strong pull on our thoughts and emotions, leading us to make choices that may not align with our true intentions. Therefore, it is important to be aware of pendulums and to detach from their influence.

Reality Transurfing also emphasizes the importance of living in the present moment and accepting the current reality without resistance. By doing so, we can let go of negative emotions and focus on positive intentions, which in turn will attract positive energy and opportunities.

Overall, Reality Transurfing offers a unique perspective on the power of our thoughts and emotions in creating our reality. It encourages us to take control of our lives by shifting our focus and intentions towards our desires, while remaining aware of the influence of external energies.

## *Poetic Recap*

*In the tapestry of existence, a path unfolds, Reality Transurfing, a story to be told. A journey of consciousness, where dreams take flight, In its subtle dance, we embrace the light.*

*Through the corridors of perception, we delve deep, Reality Transurfing, its secrets we keep. In the choices we make, in thoughts we design, We mold our own reality, in the grand design.*

*Transurfing invites us to navigate the stream, To surf the waves of life, like a vivid dream. To step beyond limits, to rewrite our story, In the realms of possibility, we find our glory.*

*In the mirror of intentions, we shape our*

*reflection, Reality Transurfing, a conscious direction. From intention to fruition, a seamless flow, In its boundless grace, our spirits aglow. Yet, it reminds us to shed our ego's cloak, To embrace the flow, in the choices we invoke. To release attachment, to outcomes and strife, In the dance of Transurfing, we sculpt our life.*

*In the concept of frames, we find the key, Reality Transurfing, where our thoughts roam free. To choose our perspective, to shift and to see, A new reality unfolding, in pure harmony.*

*So, let us embark on this conscious ride, Reality Transurfing, in our hearts reside. With intention and focus, we chart our way, In the world of limitless possibilities, we sway.*

*In the grand mosaic of life's grand parade, Reality Transurfing, where dreams cascade. With each thought we choose, and each action we take, In its sacred embrace, a new world does wake.*

*A journey of awareness, a cosmic invitation, Reality Transurfing, our conscious creation. In its gentle guidance, we find our true self, In the realms of Transurfing, we find boundless wealth.*

# Tuning to a Higher Vibration

Reality Transurfing is a popular book written by Vadim Zeland that discusses the concept of tuning into a higher vibration to attract the reality that you want. According to the author, everything in the universe is energy and operates on different frequencies or vibrations. If you can tune your energy to a higher vibration, you can attract the reality that matches that frequency. In this article, we will discuss the concept of tuning to a higher vibration and how it can help you achieve your goals.

## What is a vibration?

Before we dive deeper into the concept of higher vibrations, let's understand what a vibration is. In physics, a vibration is a repeated back-and-forth motion of an object.

Everything in the universe is made up of atoms and molecules that are in a constant state of motion, and this motion creates energy that can be measured as a frequency or vibration.

When you think of a vibration, think of a radio station. Each station has a specific frequency that it operates on, and if you tune your radio to that frequency, you can listen to that station. In the same way, everything in the universe operates on a specific frequency or vibration, and if you can tune your energy to match that frequency, you can attract the reality that matches it.

## What is a higher vibration?

A higher vibration is a frequency or energy that is associated with positive emotions such as love, joy, peace, and gratitude. When you are in a state of higher vibration, you feel more alive, happy, and fulfilled. You attract positive experiences and opportunities into your life, and everything seems to flow effortlessly.

On the other hand, a lower vibration is associated with negative emotions such as fear, anger, frustration, and sadness. When you are in a state of lower vibration, you feel drained, exhausted, and stressed. You attract negative experiences and obstacles into your life, and everything seems to be a struggle.

## How to tune to a higher vibration?

Now that we understand what a vibration is and what a higher vibration is, let's discuss how you can tune your energy to a higher vibration.

1. **Practice gratitude:** Gratitude is one of the most powerful emotions that can help you tune to a higher vibration. When you focus

on what you are grateful for, you attract more positive experiences into your life. Take a few minutes each day to write down the things you are grateful for, and feel the positive emotions associated with them.

2. **Practice mindfulness:** Mindfulness is the practice of being present in the moment and paying attention to your thoughts and feelings. When you are mindful, you can observe your thoughts without judgment and choose to focus on positive ones. Mindfulness can help you tune to a higher vibration and attract positive experiences into your life.
3. **Surround yourself with positivity:** The people you surround yourself with can have a significant impact on your vibration. If you surround yourself with negative people, you will attract negative experiences into your life. Surround yourself with positive, uplifting people who support your goals and aspirations.

4. **Visualize your goals:** Visualization is a powerful tool that can help you tune to a higher vibration. When you visualize your goals, you create a mental image of what you want to achieve. This mental image can help you attract the reality that matches it.
5. **Take care of yourself:** Taking care of yourself is essential for tuning to a higher vibration. Eat healthy foods, exercise regularly, get enough sleep, and take time to do things you enjoy. When you take care of yourself, you feel more positive and energized, and you attract positive experiences into your life.

In conclusion, tuning to a higher vibration is a powerful concept that can help you achieve your goals and attract the reality you want. By practicing gratitude, mindfulness, surrounding yourself with positivity, visualizing your goals, and taking care of yourself,you can raise your vibration and attract more positive experiences into your life. Remember that everything in the universe is energy, and by tuning your energy to a higher vibration, you can align yourself with the reality you want to create.

# *Poetic Recap*

*In the melody of life, I've come to find, A higher vibration, in the realms of the mind. It's a cosmic dance, where we all belong, In the symphony of existence, we find our song.*

*Tuning to a higher frequency, it's a notion so dear, In this grand journey of life, let me make it clear. It's a movement of love, where we all can play, In the tapestry of the universe, every single day.*

*In the eyes of a child, I've seen the truth, A higher vibration, the fountain of youth. In innocence and wonder, they teach us the way, To tune to the frequency of joy, every single day.*

*In the power of love, the world can heal, A higher vibration, it's what we all feel. In kindness and compassion, we find our grace, Tuning to love's frequency, in every embrace.*

*In the beauty of nature, a sacred design, A higher vibration, in every tree and vine. In the rustling leaves and the singing bird's call, We tune to the earth's rhythm, feeling so small.*

*In the music of the heart, I've found my guide, A higher vibration, where emotions collide. In the lyrics and chords, I hear the call, To tune to the frequency of love, one and all.*

*So let us come together, in harmony's embrace, A higher vibration, in this sacred space. In unity and peace, we find our elation, Tuning to a higher vibration, a cosmic revelation.*

*In the dance of life, let's find our way, A higher vibration, in each moment we sway. In the end, it's love that will lead us home, Tuning to love's frequency, no need to roam.*

*In the tapestry of existence, let us unite, A higher vibration, in the cosmic light. In the language of love, our hearts shall converse, Tuning to a higher vibration, let it be our universe.*

## Sound Healing

Healing sound frequencies, often referred to as sound therapy or sound healing, have gained increasing recognition for their potential to promote well-being and holistic healing. Rooted in ancient traditions and embraced by modern science, the practice involves using specific frequencies and vibrations to influence the body's energy systems, leading to physical, emotional, and spiritual balance. Central to this approach is the concept of hertz leveling for vibrational tuning, a process that aims to align the body's frequencies with optimal states for healing and elevated consciousness.

The Power of Sound Frequencies: Sound has been a fundamental element of human existence since time immemorial. Indigenous cultures have used chanting, singing bowls, drums, and other sonic tools to induce altered states of consciousness and facilitate healing. In recent years, scientific research has shed light on the intricate relationship between sound frequencies and the human body.

Every part of our body, from cells to organs, vibrates at a specific frequency. When these frequencies are disrupted or imbalanced, it can lead to physical or emotional disharmony. Healing sound frequencies are believed to restore balance by entraining the body's vibrations to healthier states. Different frequencies are associated with various effects: some promote relaxation, others stimulate energy flow, and still, others can help release emotional blockages.

Hertz Leveling for Vibrational Tuning: Hertz leveling, also known as frequency leveling, involves using specific sound frequencies to tune the body's vibrational patterns. This concept is based on the understanding that different frequencies have different effects on the body and mind. The practice often incorporates the use of sound-producing instruments like singing bowls, tuning forks, gongs, and even human voice to generate therapeutic vibrations.

One of the most well-known frequencies used in healing is the Solfeggio scale, which consists of six tones: 396 Hz, 417 Hz, 528 Hz, 639 Hz, 741 Hz, and 852 Hz. Each frequency is associated with a specific intention, such as releasing fear, enhancing creativity, and promoting spiritual growth. The idea is that exposing oneself to these frequencies through listening or direct application can recalibrate the body's energy centers, promoting self-healing and transformation.

Benefits of Using Sound Frequencies for High

Vibration: Entering a high vibrational state is often described as being in a state of resonance with positive emotions, creativity, and spiritual connectedness. Healing sound frequencies can facilitate this process by offering several notable benefits:

- Stress Reduction and Relaxation: Sound therapy can induce a state of deep relaxation, which helps reduce stress and anxiety. When the body is relaxed, it can naturally shift to higher vibrational frequencies associated with calm and well-being.
- Emotional Release: Certain sound frequencies are believed to help release emotional blockages and trauma stored in the body. As these emotional burdens are released, individuals may experience a sense of liberation and emotional lightness.
- Chakra Balancing: Sound frequencies are often used to balance and

align the body's chakra system. Each chakra is associated with specific frequencies, and using sound therapy can help clear any imbalances, allowing energy to flow freely and raising overall vibrational frequency.

- Enhanced Meditation and Mindfulness: Sound frequencies can deepen meditation and mindfulness practices. The soothing sounds create a conducive environment for entering states of deep concentration, introspection, and spiritual awareness.
- Pain Management: Sound therapy has been reported to alleviate physical pain and discomfort. By targeting specific frequencies to areas of the body experiencing pain, individuals may experience relief and a restoration of harmony.
- Improved Sleep: Listening to calming sound frequencies before sleep can help improve sleep quality. The vibrations induce relaxation and promote a sense of

tranquility, helping the body transition to a restful state.

- Enhanced Creativity and Intuition: High vibrational states are often associated with heightened creativity and intuitive insights. Sound frequencies can help individuals tap into their innate creativity and access higher levels of inspiration.
- Spiritual Growth and Awakening: Many practitioners of sound therapy report experiencing a greater sense of spiritual connection and awakening. The harmonizing effects of healing frequencies can support individuals on their spiritual journeys.

Incorporating healing sound frequencies into your daily routine can be done through various methods. You can listen to recorded sound healing sessions, attend live sound baths, or even explore using sound-generating instruments at home. It's important to note that individual experiences may vary, and sound therapy is not a replacement for medical treatment.

In conclusion, healing sound frequencies and the concept of hertz leveling offer a compelling approach to enhancing well-being and raising vibrational states. By using specific sound frequencies to entrain the body's vibrations and align with higher states of consciousness, individuals can experience a range of physical, emotional, and spiritual benefits. Whether you seek stress reduction, emotional release, spiritual growth, or improved creativity, sound therapy provides a versatile and accessible tool for elevating your overall vibrational frequency and embracing a more harmonious existence.

# *Poetic Recap*

*In the realm of vibrations, a healing grace,*
*Resides the magic of sound, in its embrace.*
*Sound healing, a symphony of the heart's desire,*
*In its gentle melodies, we find the fire.*

*In the heart's quiet chambers, where whispers reside, Sound healing unveils what we try to hide. With every note and rhythm, it gently unfolds, The stories in our souls, the secrets it holds.*

*From singing bowls to nature's sweet song, Sound healing carries us, where we belong. In the resonance of sound, we find our peace, As inner turmoil and worries release.*

*In the heart's gentle cadence, a healing refrain,*
*Sound healing soothes the spirit's silent pain.*

*With every harmonious chord, a balm for the soul, In the tapestry of healing, it plays its role.*

*In the vibrations of music, we find our way, Sound healing guides us through night and day. With melodies of hope and rhythms of grace, In its loving embrace, we find our place.*

*But sound healing's power is more than just sound, It's the connection within, where love is found. In the language of vibrations, hearts unite, In the healing symphony, we take flight.*

*So, let us honor the gift of sound's embrace, Sound healing's power, in this sacred space. With open hearts and spirits aligned, In the world of healing, we are divinely entwined.*

*In the grand orchestra of life's grand design, Sound healing, a melody both yours and mine. With each healing note, each soothing sound, In the realm of sound healing, our spirits are bound.*

# What is Energy Clearing?

Spiritual practices for clearing energy are a set of techniques that aim to remove negative or stagnant energy from the body, mind, and soul. These practices have been used for centuries by spiritual practitioners around the world to maintain a healthy energy balance and promote well-being.

1. **Meditation:**

Meditation is a powerful tool for clearing energy. It helps to calm the mind, relax the body, and reduce stress. When we meditate, we allow ourselves to become more aware of our thoughts and emotions, which can help us to identify negative patterns and release them.

2. **Yoga:**

Yoga is a physical, mental, and spiritual practice that originated in ancient India. It involves a series of postures and breathing exercises that help to balance and energize the body. Yoga can be a powerful tool for clearing energy because it helps to release tension and increase flexibility, allowing energy to flow more freely.

3. **Chakra clearing:**

The chakras are energy centers in the body that are located along the spine. There are seven chakras, each with its own unique properties and functions. When these chakras are blocked or out of balance, it can lead to physical, emotional, and spiritual imbalances. Chakra clearing involves using various techniques such as visualization, meditation, and sound therapy to remove blockages and restore balance.

### 4. Reiki:

Reiki is a form of energy healing that originated in Japan. It involves the use of the hands to channel energy into the body, helping to promote healing and balance. Reiki can be a powerful tool for clearing energy because it can help to release blocked energy and restore balance to the body, mind, and soul.

### 5. Smudging:

Smudging is a traditional Native American practice that involves burning herbs such as sage, cedar, or sweetgrass to purify the air and remove negative energy. The smoke from the herbs is believed to carry away negative energy and bring in positive energy.

6. **Sound therapy:**

Sound therapy involves using sound vibrations to promote healing and balance. This can include listening to music, chanting, or using sound bowls or tuning forks. Sound therapy can be a powerful tool for clearing energy because it can help to release tension and promote relaxation.

7. **Mindfulness:**

Mindfulness involves being present in the moment and paying attention to our thoughts and emotions without judgment. It can help us to become more aware of negative thought patterns and release them. Mindfulness can be a powerful tool for clearing energy because it helps us to become more aware of our energy and the impact that our thoughts and emotions have on it.

In conclusion, spiritual practices for clearing energy are a set of powerful tools that can help us to maintain a healthy energy balance and promote well-being. By incorporating these practices into our daily lives, we can learn to release negative energy and promote positive energy flow, leading to greater health and vitality. Whether we choose to practice yoga, meditation, or sound therapy, there are many ways to clear our energy and promote a healthy, balanced life.

## *Poetic Recap*

*In the depths of our being, where shadows reside, Lies the art of energy clearing, like a gentle tide. A sacred practice to release what's confined, In the realm of the spirit, where light's designed.*

*With intention and focus, we begin the quest, Energy clearing, where hearts find rest. To cleanse the soul of what no longer serves, In the dance of release, the spirit observes.*

*Like a breath of fresh air, a cleansing breeze, Energy clearing sets the spirit at ease. From burdens to worries, they melt away, In the flow of healing, we find our way.*

*In the corners of consciousness, where emotions accrue, Energy clearing unearths what's hidden from view. To release the old stories and patterns of old, In the healing journey, we find ourselves bold.*

*With sage or with crystals, with chants or with prayer, Energy clearing, a practice so rare. To purify the aura, to cleanse the heart's core, In the realm of energy, we restore and explore.*

*In the embrace of nature, where elements sway, Energy clearing, like the light of day. In forests and oceans, where purity gleams, We cleanse our spirits in the natural streams.*

*But energy clearing is more than just sage, It's a mindful practice, in every life stage. With forgiveness and love, we find the key, To release and let go, to set our hearts free.*

*So, let us embark on this sacred art, Energy clearing, where healing does impart. With each intention we set, each negative cord, In the dance of clearing, our spirits restored.*

*In the grand tapestry of life's grand parade, Energy clearing, where serenity's cascade. With each breath we take, in this journey we're nearing, In the world of energy, there's endless clearing.*

# Blowing Roses Meditation

Blowing roses is a form of meditation that can help individuals to become more mindful, focused, and present in their daily lives. This type of meditation involves visualizing the act of blowing a rose, which can help to reduce stress and promote relaxation.

To begin the meditation, it is important to find a quiet and comfortable space where you can sit and focus. You may want to light a candle or incense to create a calming atmosphere, and it can also be helpful to take a few deep breaths to center yourself and quiet your mind.

Once you are ready to begin, close your eyes and visualize a rose in your mind. Imagine that you are holding the rose in your hand, and take a moment to observe its beauty and fragrance. Then, imagine that you are blowing on the rose, gently releasing its petals into the air.

As you blow on the rose, focus your attention on your breath and the sensation of the air moving through your body. Allow yourself to become fully absorbed in the act of blowing on the rose, and let go of any thoughts or distractions that may arise.

As you continue to blow on the rose, you may notice that your mind begins to quiet and your body relaxes. This is because the act of blowing on the rose can help to regulate your breathing, which in turn can help to reduce stress and promote relaxation.

You may choose to repeat the visualization of blowing on the rose several times during your meditation, or you may simply focus on it for a few moments before moving on to another form of meditation.

In addition to promoting relaxation and reducing stress, blowing roses can also help to cultivate a sense of gratitude and appreciation for the beauty of the world around us. By visualizing the act of blowing on a rose, we are reminded of the fragility and impermanence of life, and we are encouraged to savor each moment as it comes.

As you practice blowing roses, you may find that it becomes easier to let go of negative thoughts and emotions, and that you are better able to focus your attention on the present moment. You may also find that you feel more connected to the natural world, and that you have a greater sense of appreciation for the simple pleasures of life.

In conclusion, blowing roses is a simple and effective form of meditation that can help individuals to become more mindful, focused, and present in their daily lives. By visualizing the act of blowing on a rose, we can reduce stress, promote relaxation, and cultivate a sense of gratitude for the beauty of the world around us. Whether you are new to meditation or have been practicing for years, blowing roses is a powerful tool that can help you to deepen your practice and find greater peace and contentment in your life.

# The Origins of Blowing Roses

The Blowing Roses Meditation is a popular visualization technique used in meditation and mindfulness practices. This meditation technique is said to help individuals develop awareness and mindfulness by focusing on the visualization of a rose and imagining the process of blowing the petals away. While the exact origin of this meditation is unknown, it has been used by practitioners for many years.

The Blowing Roses Meditation is said to have originated in the East, where meditation and mindfulness practices have been a part of daily life for centuries. In Eastern cultures, mindfulness is considered a way of life, and many meditation practices are taught from a young age. It is believed that the Blowing Roses Meditation was passed down from generation to generation through the teachings of mindfulness and meditation.

In the Western world, the Blowing Roses Meditation gained popularity in the 1970s and 1980s as part of the New Age movement. This movement focused on spiritual and personal growth, and many people turned to meditation as a way to achieve inner peace and balance. The Blowing Roses Meditation became a popular technique because it was easy to learn, and the visualization of a rose made it easy to focus the mind.

The exact origin of the Blowing Roses Meditation is difficult to pinpoint because it has been adapted and modified over the years. However, many experts agree that the visualization of the rose is symbolic of the human experience. The rose represents the beauty and fragility of life, while the blowing of the petals symbolizes the impermanence of all things.

In the Blowing Roses Meditation, the practitioner is instructed to imagine a rose in front of them. They then visualize themselves blowing the petals off the rose one by one. As they blow the petals away, they are encouraged to let go of negative thoughts and emotions and focus on the present moment. The process of blowing the petals away is said to help individuals release attachments and let go of the past.

The Blowing Roses Meditation has been used to help individuals cope with stress, anxiety, and depression. It is a simple technique that can be practiced by anyone, regardless of their level of experience with meditation. The visualization of the rose is easy to remember, and the blowing of the petals provides a physical sensation that can help individuals focus their minds.

In conclusion, the origin of the Blowing Roses Meditation is unknown, but it has been used by practitioners for many years. It is believed to have originated in the East and was passed down through the teachings of mindfulness and meditation. In the Western world, the Blowing Roses Meditation gained popularity in the 1970s and 1980s as part of the New Age movement. The visualization of the rose is symbolic of the human experience, and the blowing of the petals represents the impermanence of all things. The Blowing Roses Meditation has been used to help individuals cope with stress, anxiety, and depression, and it is a simple technique that can be practiced by anyone.

## *Poetic Recap*

*In the garden of tranquility, we find our reprieve, With a meditation known as "Blowing Roses," we believe. A practice to calm the mind and soothe the soul, In the world of inner peace, we find our ultimate goal.*

*Close your eyes, dear soul, let the chaos subside,*
*In the realms of meditation, let your spirit glide.*
*Imagine a garden, where fragrant roses bloom,*
*Their petals soft whispers, in the silent room.*

*As you breathe in deeply, the scent of the rose,*
*Feel your body relaxing, your worries it slows.*
*With each inhalation, a rosebud unfurls, In the Blowing Roses meditation, serenity swirls.*

*Now imagine a rose in the palm of your hand,*

*Its color and fragrance, so vividly grand. As you exhale gently, release the rose's sweet breath, In this meditation's embrace, find freedom from death.*

*Inhale and embrace, the rose's gentle bloom, Exhale and let go, release all your gloom. With each breath you take, let the roses cascade, In this garden of peace, let your spirit upgrade. With each breath in and out, find your rhythm and flow, In the Blowing Roses meditation, let your worries go. With the roses as guides, you'll find your own way, To inner serenity, where your heart can sway.*

*As you continue this journey, your mind becomes clear, In the fragrance of roses, you have nothing to fear. With each breath and each rose, a deeper peace you'll find, In the Blowing Roses meditation, tranquility enshrined.*

*When you're ready to return, from this sacred*

*retreat, Carry the roses' essence, in your heart, it's complete. In the world of meditation, you've discovered the way, To find peace and stillness, in each passing day.*

*So, let the Blowing Roses guide you to grace, In this meditation's garden, find your sacred space. With each breath and each bloom, may your spirit be at ease, In the Blowing Roses meditation, find your inner peace.*

## The Law of Inspiration

The Law of Inspiration is a concept that has been discussed and debated by many individuals throughout history. The idea behind this law is that humans can tap into a higher source of knowledge or creativity beyond their conscious awareness, which allows them to produce works of art, literature, music, and scientific breakthroughs that they couldn't have created on their own. In this essay, we'll delve into the concept of the Law of Inspiration, its history, and how it applies to various fields.

The Law of Inspiration has its roots in religious and spiritual traditions. Many cultures throughout history have attributed the creation of art and other forms of human creativity to divine intervention. For instance, in Ancient

Greece, the Muses were believed to be the source of inspiration for artists and writers. Similarly, in the Bible, it is said that the Holy Spirit inspired the prophets to speak the word of God.

In more modern times, the concept of the Law of Inspiration has been explored by various philosophers and scientists. One of the most notable proponents of this idea was Carl Jung, who believed that human creativity was the result of tapping into the collective unconscious, a deeper layer of the mind that contains the wisdom and experiences of all humanity. Jung argued that artists and other creative individuals were able to access this collective unconscious through dreams, intuition, and other forms of inspiration.

Similarly, the psychologist Abraham Maslow proposed the concept of self-actualization, which involves realizing one's full potential and achieving a state of personal fulfillment. Maslow believed that individuals who reached this state were able to tap into a higher level of consciousness, which allowed them to create works of art, literature, and music that were truly inspired.

The Law of Inspiration is not limited to the arts, however. It also applies to scientific breakthroughs and innovations. Many scientists and inventors have reported that their best ideas came to them in moments of inspiration, often when they were not actively working on the problem they were trying to solve. For instance, Albert Einstein claimed that his theory of relativity came to him in a dream, while Archimedes is said to have had his eureka moment while taking a bath.

In business and entrepreneurship, the Law of Inspiration can be seen in the concept of "thinking outside the box." Many successful entrepreneurs and business leaders have been able to achieve great success by tapping into their intuition and coming up with innovative ideas that challenge conventional wisdom. Steve Jobs, for instance, famously encouraged his team at Apple to "think different" and pursue bold ideas that others might have dismissed as impossible.

The Law of Inspiration has also been explored in the context of personal growth and self-improvement. Many individuals who have achieved great success in their careers or personal lives have attributed their success to a moment of inspiration or insight that allowed them to see things in a new way. By tapping into this higher source of knowledge, they were able to overcome obstacles and achieve their goals.

In conclusion, the Law of Inspiration is a powerful concept that has been explored by many individuals throughout history. Whether in the arts, sciences, business, or personal growth, the ability to tap into a higher source of knowledge or creativity can lead to breakthroughs and innovations that would have otherwise been impossible. While the concept of the Law of Inspiration may be difficult to quantify or measure, its impact on human creativity and achievement cannot be denied.

# *Poetic Recap*

*In the tapestry of life's grand design, Resides the law of inspiration, a force divine. A guiding light that sparks the creative fire, In the realm of the soul's deepest desire.*

*From the whispers of nature to the artist's brush, Inspiration is the river in which we rush. A muse that dances in the poet's pen, In the law of inspiration, we're reborn again.*

*In the heart's silent chambers, where dreams reside, Inspiration stirs the embers, takes us on a ride. It's the call to action, the creative flame, In the world of inspiration, we stake our claim. From the music that moves us to the stories that bind, Inspiration fuels the imagination's mind. In melodies and verses, it finds its home, In the law of inspiration, we ceaselessly roam.*

*But inspiration's gift is not just for the few, It resides in us all, a universal view. In the beauty of life, the connections we make, In the law of inspiration, our spirits awake.*

*In the moments of stillness, in nature's embrace, Inspiration unveils its tender grace. With every breath we take, in the silence we find, In the world of inspiration, our souls intertwined.*

*So, let us honor this law, in heart and in thought, Inspiration's wisdom, let it be sought. With open hearts and spirits aligned, In the realm of inspiration, our dreams defined.*

*In the grand symphony of life's grand parade, Inspiration, a melody both quiet and brave. With each spark of insight, each creative sensation, In the law of inspiration, find your divine foundation.*

*In the dance of creation, let inspiration be your guide, In its radiant embrace, let your dreams take their stride. With every inspired thought, with every elation, In the law of inspiration, find your true salvation.*

## What is FLOW?

The concept of flow is an idea developed by Dr. Mihaly Csikszentmihalyi, a Hungarian-American psychologist, who coined the term "flow" to describe a state of optimal experience in which people are fully absorbed in a task or activity. Flow is a psychological state in which individuals feel completely absorbed in their work, feeling energized, focused, and fully immersed in the task at hand. In this state, individuals lose track of time, forget about their surroundings, and are fully engaged in the present moment.

Dr. Malik has further expanded upon Csikszentmihalyi's work and has introduced the concept of "Flow in Action." According to Dr. Malik, flow in action is a state of mind in which individuals experience the joy and satisfaction of being fully present and engaged in what they are doing. This state is characterized by a sense of effortlessness, heightened awareness, and a feeling of being in control.

To achieve flow in action, Dr. Malik identifies four key elements: clarity of purpose, skill mastery, feedback, and challenge. Clarity of purpose refers to having a clear understanding of the goals and objectives of the task at hand. Skill mastery involves having the necessary skills and expertise to complete the task successfully. Feedback is essential for providing individuals with information on their performance and progress, which allows them to adjust their approach and improve their results. Lastly, challenge refers to the level of difficulty or complexity of the task. The challenge should be significant enough to push individuals beyond their comfort zone but not so difficult that it becomes overwhelming.

When these four elements are present, individuals are able to achieve a state of flow in action, which has numerous benefits. Flow in action can lead to increased productivity, creativity, and innovation. When individuals are in a state of flow, they are fully focused on the task at hand, and their minds are free from distractions. This allows them to perform at their highest level and produce exceptional results. In addition, flow in action can lead to increased job satisfaction, as individuals are more engaged and fulfilled by their work.

Dr. Malik also emphasizes the importance of mindfulness in achieving flow in action. Mindfulness involves being fully present in the moment and aware of one's thoughts, feelings, and surroundings. When individuals are mindful, they are better able to focus on the task at hand and avoid distractions. Mindfulness can also help individuals to regulate their emotions and reduce stress, which can further enhance their ability to achieve flow in action.

In summary, flow is a state of mind in which individuals are fully engaged in a task or activity, and flow in action is a state of optimal experience that is characterized by clarity of purpose, skill mastery, feedback, and challenge. Achieving flow in action can lead to increased productivity, creativity, and innovation, as well as increased job satisfaction. Mindfulness is also an essential component of achieving flow in action, as it helps individuals to stay focused, regulate their emotions, and reduce stress. By understanding and applying the concept of flow in action, individuals can enhance their performance and experience greater fulfillment in their work and daily lives.

# *FLOW* STATE

Flow states, also known as being "in the zone," are states of high performance and intense focus that can help individuals achieve their goals and find greater satisfaction in their lives. Living in a flow state can lead to greater creativity, productivity, and fulfillment. There are several principles that can help individuals achieve and maintain a state of flow.

### 1. Set Clear Goals

Setting clear goals is the first step in achieving a state of flow. When goals are defined, it is easier to focus attention and energy on the task at hand. Clear goals provide a sense of direction and purpose, and can help to reduce distractions and feelings of overwhelm. Goals should be specific, measurable, achievable, relevant, and time-bound (SMART). When goals are SMART, they become more meaningful and motivating.

### 2. Focus on the Present Moment

Flow states require a complete focus on the present moment. It is essential to let go of past failures and future worries and fully immerse oneself in the task at hand. When the mind is fully focused on the present, distractions are reduced, and attention is maximized. One way to focus on the present moment is through mindfulness practices, such as meditation or deep breathing exercises.

### 3. Cultivate Positive Emotions

Positive emotions are essential for living

in a flow state. Positive emotions such as joy, excitement, and enthusiasm can help to increase motivation and creativity, and decrease feelings of anxiety and stress. Cultivating positive emotions requires individuals to recognize and acknowledge their emotions, and actively seek out activities and experiences that elicit positive emotions.

### 4. Seek Out Challenging Tasks

Flow states require tasks that are challenging but achievable. When tasks are too easy, individuals can become bored, and when tasks are too difficult, they can become overwhelmed. Challenging tasks provide a sense of excitement and engagement, and can help individuals to achieve a state of flow. When individuals engage in challenging tasks, they are more likely to experience a sense of accomplishment and mastery.

## 5. Embrace Failure as a Learning Opportunity

Failure is an inevitable part of life, but it can be a valuable learning opportunity. When individuals embrace failure as an opportunity to learn and grow, they are more likely to persist in the face of challenges and setbacks. Failure can provide valuable feedback and help individuals to refine their approach to achieving their goals. When individuals view failure as a natural part of the learning process, they are more likely to bounce back and continue striving towards their goals.

## 6. Practice Self-Care

Self-care is essential for living in a flow state. When individuals prioritize their physical and emotional well-being, they are better able to manage stress and maintain a positive mindset.

Self-care practices can include activities such as exercise, meditation, socializing, and getting enough sleep. Practicing self-care can help individuals to maintain their energy levels and stay focused and engaged in their activities.

In conclusion, living in a flow state requires a combination of goal-setting, present-moment focus, positive emotions, challenging tasks, embracing failure, and self-care. When individuals adopt these principles, they can achieve a state of flow, which can lead to increased productivity, creativity, and overall life satisfaction.

# *Poetic Recap*

*In the river of time, where moments cascade, Resides the magic of flow, where spirits are swayed. A state of being, both timeless and free, In the dance of the present, we find the key.*

*Flow is a river, winding its way, Through the heart's landscape, where passions sway. In the zone of creation, where artists take flight, In the world of flow, all is pure and bright.*

*With focus and purpose, we enter the stream, In the realm of the flow, we find our dream. Each action a brushstroke, each thought a refrain, In the flow state, we break every chain.*

*Time becomes fluid, as hours slip away, In the embrace of flow, we joyfully sway. Effort and action blend seamlessly together, In the dance of flow, we find our endeavor.*

*From athletes to artists, from thinkers to doers, Flow is the magic that ignites our pursuits. In the space of surrender, where ego's set free, In the flow state, we're as boundless as the sea.*

*But flow's not a gift for the chosen few, It's a state of existence, available to you. With presence and practice, it becomes our guide, In the world of the flow, we let go of our pride.*

*In the grand design of life's grand parade, Flow is the current, where dreams are remade. With each breath we take, with each moment we treasure, In the state of the flow, we find boundless pleasure.*

*So, let us honor this state, with hearts open wide, In the flow of existence, we find our stride. With passion and purpose, we'll forever create,*

*In the world of the flow, our destinies await.*

*In the symphony of life, where moments unfold, Flow is the melody, both precious and bold. With each step we take, with each choice we embrace, In the flow state, we find our sacred space.*

## Manifesting Revisited

The concept of manifesting is a term that has gained popularity in contemporary culture, especially in the realm of self-help and spirituality. Manifesting is the belief that individuals can bring their desires and goals into existence by using the power of their thoughts, emotions, and actions. The concept of manifesting is based on the idea that the universe is made up of energy and that our thoughts and emotions are forms of energy that can attract or repel certain experiences or outcomes.

The term "manifesting" is derived from the word "manifest," which means to make something visible or apparent. In the context of manifesting, it means bringing a desired outcome into existence by focusing one's thoughts, emotions, and actions on that outcome. The belief is that the universe will respond to these focused intentions and bring the desired outcome into reality.

The concept of manifesting has been used in various forms throughout history. Ancient cultures, such as the Egyptians, Greeks, and Romans, believed in the power of manifestation and used rituals and spells to bring about desired outcomes. In modern times, the concept has been popularized by the New Age movement and self-help gurus such as Esther Hicks, Wayne Dyer, and Rhonda Byrne.

The basic premise of manifesting is that individuals can use the power of their thoughts and emotions to attract positive experiences and outcomes into their lives. According to the law of attraction, like attracts like, and therefore, positive thoughts and emotions will attract positive experiences, while negative thoughts and emotions will attract negative experiences.

The process of manifesting typically involves several steps. The first step is to identify a specific goal or desire that one wishes to manifest. This could be anything from a new job, a romantic relationship, or improved health. The next step is to visualize the desired outcome as if it has already been achieved. This involves using all of one's senses to create a vivid mental image of the desired outcome.

The third step is to focus one's thoughts and emotions on the desired outcome. This involves cultivating a positive and optimistic mindset and using affirmations and positive self-talk to reinforce the belief that the desired outcome is possible. The fourth step is to take inspired action towards the desired outcome. This involves taking practical steps towards achieving the goal, such as networking, sending out resumes, or going on dates.

Manifesting has become a popular concept in contemporary culture, particularly in the realm of self-help and spirituality. The idea of manifesting has been popularized by books such as "The Secret" by Rhonda Byrne, which promotes the concept of the law of attraction and encourages readers to focus their thoughts and emotions on positive outcomes.

The popularity of manifesting has also led to the development of various manifestation tools and techniques. These include vision boards, which involve creating a collage of images that represent the desired outcome, and gratitude journals, which involve writing down things that one is grateful for in order to cultivate a positive mindset.

Manifesting has also become a popular topic on social media, with hashtags such as #manifesting and #lawofattraction trending on platforms such as Instagram and TikTok. Influencers and celebrities have also jumped on the manifesting bandwagon, sharing their own manifestation success stories and promoting manifestation techniques and products.

Critics of the concept of manifesting argue that it promotes a magical thinking mindset and encourages people to focus on unrealistic goals and desires. They also argue that it can be harmful to those who are struggling with serious issues such as poverty, illness, or trauma, as it can imply that these issues are the result of negative thinking or lack of effort.

In conclusion, the concept of manifesting is a popular idea in contemporary culture, particularly in the realm of self-help and spirituality. Manifesting involves using the power of one's thoughts, emotions, and actions to bring desired outcomes into reality. While manifesting has its critics, proponents argue that it can be a powerful tool for personal growth and achieving one's goals. The belief in manifesting is based on the idea that individuals have agency over their lives and can create their own reality through their thoughts and emotions.

The concept of manifesting also emphasizes the importance of positive thinking and cultivating a positive mindset. This can be beneficial for individuals who struggle with negative self-talk or low self-esteem, as it encourages them to focus on their strengths and possibilities for growth.

Ultimately, the concept of manifesting is a personal belief and practice that can vary from individual to individual. While it may not work for everyone, those who believe in manifesting find it to be a powerful tool for achieving their goals and creating positive change in their lives.

# The Kybalion Revisited

The Kybalion is a well-known text in the field of Hermetic philosophy, which explores the principles and practices of the ancient Egyptian mystery schools. Hermetic philosophy is based on the teachings of the mythical figure Hermes Trismegistus, who is said to have lived in ancient Egypt around 3000 BCE. The Kybalion is believed to have been written by three initiates of the Hermetic philosophy who chose to remain anonymous, and it serves as a guide to the principles and practices of this ancient tradition.

Hermetic philosophy is deeply connected to ancient Egypt, as it is believed to have originated in the mystery schools of this civilization. The ancient Egyptians were known for their profound wisdom and understanding of the universe, and their teachings had a significant impact on the development of philosophy and science in the ancient world. One of the key figures in the transmission of this wisdom was the god Thoth, who was believed to have brought knowledge and wisdom to the people of Egypt.

Thoth was also known as Hermes Trismegistus, which means "Thrice-Great Hermes," and he was considered the founder of Hermetic philosophy. According to legend, Hermes Trismegistus was a powerful sage who possessed a deep understanding of the universe and its workings. He was said to have written numerous texts on the subject, which were later compiled into a single volume known as the Corpus Hermeticum.

The Corpus Hermeticum was a collection of texts that explored the principles and practices of Hermetic philosophy. These texts covered a wide range of topics, from cosmology and metaphysics to alchemy and magic. They were written in a poetic and symbolic language that was meant to be interpreted by initiates of the Hermetic tradition, rather than understood literally.

One of the key principles of Hermetic philosophy was the concept of correspondence, which stated that there was a correspondence between the various levels of reality. This meant that the principles that governed the physical world also governed the spiritual and mental worlds, and that by understanding these principles, one could gain insight into the workings of the universe as a whole.

Another important principle of Hermetic philosophy was the idea of polarity, which stated that everything in the universe had its opposite. This meant that light had darkness, good had evil, and so on. However, Hermetic philosophy also emphasized that these opposites were not separate and distinct, but rather two aspects of a single unified whole.

The Kybalion, which was written in the early 20th century, is considered one of the most important texts in the field of Hermetic philosophy. It was written by three initiates of the Hermetic tradition who chose to remain anonymous, and it served as a guide to the principles and practices of this ancient tradition.

The Kybalion covers many of the same principles and concepts found in the Corpus Hermeticum, but it presents them in a more accessible and modern language. It also expands on some of the ideas found in the earlier texts, such as the concept of vibration, which states that everything in the universe is in a constant state of vibration.

The Kybalion also explores the concept of mentalism, which states that the universe is a mental creation, and that everything that exists is a product of the mind. This idea is rooted in the ancient Egyptian belief in the power of the mind to create reality, and it was later explored in depth by the New Thought movement in the late 19th and early 20th centuries.

Overall, the Kybalion and Hermetic philosophy are deeply connected to ancient Egypt and its teachings. Through the writings of figures like Hermes Trismegistus and Thoth, this ancient wisdom was passed down through the ages, and it continues to inspire and inform spiritual seekers to this day.

# *Poetic Recap*

*In the mystic scrolls of wisdom's ancient lore, Lies the Kybalion, teachings to explore. A sacred text, a cosmic key, Unveiling truths of the universe, for all to see.*

*As above, so below, its message does proclaim, In the Kybalion's verses, we find our aim. The seven principles, a spiritual map, In the journey of the soul, they bridge the gap.*

*The first, the Principle of Mentalism, so clear, All is mind, the universe's frontier. In the grand cosmic scheme, thoughts create, In the Kybalion's wisdom, we contemplate.*

*The Principle of Correspondence, the second in line, As above, so below, in the divine design.*

*In the micro and macro, patterns entwine, In the Kybalion's guidance, we seek the divine.*

*The Principle of Vibration, a cosmic dance, Everything is energy, in the universe's expanse. In the rhythms of life, in each pulse and flow, In the Kybalion's verses, we come to know.*

*The fourth, the Principle of Polarity, we find, In duality's embrace, the soul is aligned. From dark to light, in the ebb and flow, In the Kybalion's teachings, we find our glow.*

*The Principle of Rhythm, the fifth in line, In cycles and seasons, life's grand design. In the dance of time, in its ebb and swell, In the Kybalion's wisdom, we find it well.*

*The Principle of Cause and Effect, the sixth to explore, As we sow, so we reap, in life's grand score. In choices we make, in each cause and effect, In the Kybalion's guidance, our lessons reflect.*

*The seventh, the Principle of Gender, we embrace, In balance and harmony, we find our grace. In the union of opposites, the cosmic blend, In the Kybalion's verses, our souls ascend. In the sacred pages of the Kybalion's lore, Ancient wisdom beckons, forevermore. A cosmic guide, a path to the divine, In its timeless teachings, our spirits entwine.*

*So, let us honor the Kybalion's call, In its seven principles, we stand tall. In the dance of existence, in the secrets it holds, In the Kybalion's wisdom, our souls find their molds.*

# What is Hermetic Philosophy

Hermetic philosophy refers to a set of philosophical and mystical beliefs that are based on the teachings of Hermes Trismegistus, an ancient Egyptian deity associated with wisdom and knowledge. The term Hermeticism was coined during the Renaissance when the rediscovery of ancient texts attributed to Hermes Trismegistus sparked renewed interest in the teachings of this enigmatic figure.

The core of Hermetic philosophy is the idea that there is a fundamental unity underlying all of existence. This unity is expressed in various ways, such as the principle of correspondence, which states that there is a correspondence between different levels of reality, such as the physical and spiritual planes. Another key principle is the concept of polarity, which suggests that everything has two opposing aspects, such as light and darkness, male and female, or positive and negative.

Hermeticism also emphasizes the power of the human mind to understand and transform the world. This is expressed in the principle of mentalism, which suggests that the universe is mental in nature, and that our thoughts and beliefs shape our reality. Hermetic philosophy also emphasizes the importance of spiritual development, and the idea that we can achieve union with the divine through spiritual practices such as meditation and contemplation.

One of the most famous works attributed to Hermes Trismegistus is the Corpus Hermeticum, a collection of texts that were written in Greek during the first few centuries

CE. The Corpus Hermeticum contains a wide range of teachings, including discussions of cosmology, theology, and ethics. Many of these teachings are expressed in the form of dialogues between Hermes and his disciple, and they often involve esoteric concepts and mystical experiences.

Hermetic philosophy has had a profound impact on Western culture, influencing the development of various mystical and esoteric traditions. The Renaissance saw a renewed interest in Hermeticism, with figures such as Marsilio Ficino and Giovanni Pico della Mirandola incorporating Hermetic ideas into their philosophical and theological writings. Hermeticism also influenced the development of alchemy, an ancient precursor to modern chemistry that sought to transform base metals into gold and achieve spiritual enlightenment through the transmutation of matter.

In the modern era, Hermetic philosophy has continued to inspire spiritual seekers and mystical thinkers. The writings of figures such as Helena Blavatsky, Aleister Crowley, and Carl Jung have all been influenced by Hermetic ideas. Hermeticism has also been a significant influence on the development of modern paganism, with many pagan practitioners incorporating Hermetic concepts and practices into their spiritual traditions.

Overall, Hermetic philosophy represents a complex and multifaceted approach to understanding the world and our place within it. Its emphasis on the unity of all things, the power of the human mind, and the importance of spiritual development has made it a significant influence on Western thought and culture. While the origins of Hermeticism remain shrouded in mystery, its teachings continue to inspire spiritual seekers and mystical thinkers to this day.

## *Poetic Recap*

*In the depths of ancient wisdom, a sacred scroll,*
*Resides Hermetic Philosophy, a treasure untold.*
*A path of enlightenment, a quest for the soul,*
*In the Hermetic teachings, we find our role.*

*As above, so below, its first principle does declare,*
*In the grand cosmic dance, we're a part to bear.*
*The microcosm reflects the macrocosm's grace, In*
*Hermetic Philosophy, we find our place.*

*The principle of correspondence, a bridge to*
*span, Between worlds above and worlds of*
*man. In patterns and cycles, it guides our quest,*
*In Hermetic teachings, we find our rest.*

*The rhythm of life, in the third principle's sway,*
*As above, so below, in the night and the day. In*
*the dance of existence, in each rise and fall, In*

*Hermetic Philosophy, we heed the call.*

*The principle of polarity, the fourth in line, In duality's embrace, the soul does shine. From dark to light, in the ebb and the flow, In Hermetic teachings, we come to know.*

*The fifth, the principle of vibration's song, Everything is energy, in the cosmic throng. In the waves of life, in each pulse and sway, In Hermetic Philosophy, we find our way.*

*Cause and effect, the sixth principle to seek, In choices we make, our destinies we speak. As we sow, so we reap, in life's grand scheme, In Hermetic teachings, we find our dream.*

*The seventh, the principle of gender, does blend, In balance and harmony, our spirits ascend. In the union of opposites, the cosmic plan, In Hermetic Philosophy, we become as one.*

*In the scrolls of Hermetic wisdom, we find the light, A path of enlightenment, in day and night. In the sacred teachings, our spirits soar, In Hermetic Philosophy, we seek forevermore.*

*So, let us honor this wisdom of old, In Hermetic Philosophy, our truths unfold. In the dance of existence, in its secrets we delve, In the Hermetic teachings, we find our true selves.*

# What is Atlantis?

The legend of Atlantis is one of the most fascinating stories in mythology. It tells the tale of a great city, built by a powerful civilization, that sank beneath the waves in a single day and night of catastrophic destruction. The story of Atlantis has been the subject of countless books, movies, and TV shows, and has captured the imaginations of people around the world for centuries. But where did this legend come from, and what are its origins?

The first written record of the Atlantis story comes from the ancient Greek philosopher Plato, who described the lost city in two of his dialogues, the Timaeus and the Critias. According to Plato, Atlantis was a great island located beyond the pillars of Hercules, which we now know as the Strait of Gibraltar. The island was said to be home to a powerful civilization that had surpassed all others in wealth, technology, and military might.

Plato's description of Atlantis is full of vivid details. He describes a network of canals and waterways that crisscrossed the island, as well as magnificent temples and palaces made of precious metals and gemstones. The people of Atlantis were said to be highly advanced, possessing knowledge of mathematics, astronomy, and engineering far beyond what was known in Plato's time.

But despite their great power and wealth, the people of Atlantis were said to have become corrupt and arrogant, and had angered the gods. In punishment, the gods sent a great flood that swept over the island, sinking it beneath the waves and destroying the civilization that had once flourished there.

The story of Atlantis has fascinated people for centuries, and has inspired countless works of literature, art, and entertainment. But where did Plato get the idea for this lost city, and is there any truth to the legend?

Some historians and archaeologists believe that the Atlantis story was inspired by real-life events. One theory suggests that Plato was describing the Minoan civilization, which flourished on the island of Crete from about 2600 BCE to 1450 BCE. The Minoans were known for their advanced technology and sophisticated culture, and were one of the most powerful civilizations in the ancient Mediterranean world. However, their civilization was destroyed by a catastrophic volcanic eruption on the island of Thera (modern-day Santorini) around 1600 BCE, which may have inspired Plato's story of a great city destroyed by a natural disaster.

Another theory suggests that the Atlantis story may have been inspired by ancient memories of the Black Sea flood, which occurred around 5600 BCE. This catastrophic event, which was caused by rising sea levels and the collapse of a natural dam, is thought to have flooded an area of land the size of Great Britain, including many coastal settlements. The Black Sea flood is thought to have inspired numerous flood myths and legends around the world, including the story of Noah's ark in the Bible.

Despite these theories, there is no conclusive evidence to support the idea that the Atlantis story was based on real-life events. Many historians and archaeologists believe that the story is simply a work of fiction, intended to illustrate Plato's ideas about the ideal society and the dangers of greed and arrogance.

Regardless of its origins, the legend of Atlantis

continues to captivate people's imaginations to this day. The idea of a lost city, with all its wealth and technology, hidden beneath the waves, is a powerful symbol of the mysteries of the past and the depths of human ambition. Whether or not Atlantis ever really existed, its legend will continue to inspire and fascinate people for generations to come.

## *Poetic Recap*

*In the mists of time, a legend does reside, Of a city called Atlantis, where the ancients did abide. A tale of grandeur, shrouded in the sea's embrace, Atlantis, a realm of mystery, in its rightful place.*

*In the heart of the ocean, this city did stand, A marvel of architecture, across the land. Its beauty and knowledge, beyond compare, In the legend of Atlantis, we're drawn to stare.*

*A civilization advanced, with wisdom so profound, In Atlantis, ancient secrets were found. Inventors and scholars, in their quest for the skies, Atlantis, a beacon of knowledge, in the world's eyes.*

*But pride and ambition, a shadow did cast,*

*Over Atlantis, a city built to last. In its hubris, it sought to reach the divine, And in doing so, it crossed a dangerous line.*

*The earth shook and trembled, the ocean's roar, Atlantis was swallowed, to be seen no more. In the depths of the sea, it lies in repose, The legend of Atlantis, where mystery grows.*

*Yet whispers persist, in tales and in dreams, Of a city that vanished, in the ocean's extremes. In the hearts of explorers, its memory does cling, The legend of Atlantis, an eternal spring.*

*In the search for knowledge, and the thirst for the past, Atlantis remains a story that forever will last. A lesson in hubris, in its rise and its fall, In the legend of Atlantis, we heed wisdom's call.*

*So, let us remember this city of old, In Atlantis' legend, its story is told. A reminder of balance, of humility and grace, In the annals of history, its memory we embrace.*

*In the mists of time, the legend still thrives, Of a city beneath the waves, where history derives. Atlantis, a mystery, in the ocean's blue, Its secrets and lessons, forever in view.*

# Atlantis and Contemporary Times

The legend of Atlantis has captured the imagination of people around the world for centuries, and its legacy can still be felt in contemporary times. While there is no conclusive evidence that Atlantis ever really existed, many people believe that the story of the lost city holds deep spiritual and metaphysical significance, and that its legacy can still be felt in our modern world.

One of the most significant spiritual connections between contemporary times and Atlantis is the idea of a lost, ancient wisdom that has been forgotten or suppressed over time. The people of Atlantis were said to possess knowledge and technology far beyond what was known in Plato's time, and many people believe that this knowledge was passed down through secret societies and mystical traditions.

Today, many spiritual seekers believe that this ancient wisdom is still available to those who seek it out, and that it holds the key to unlocking the full potential of human consciousness. This idea has given rise to a variety of spiritual and metaphysical practices, including meditation, yoga, and energy healing, which are often seen as ways to connect with this ancient wisdom and tap into the power of the universe.

Another spiritual connection between contemporary times and Atlantis is the idea of a lost paradise, a utopian society that existed in a golden age before the corruption and degradation of modern times. The people of Atlantis were said to live in a perfect society, where everyone was equal and all needs were met. Many spiritual seekers today believe that this utopian vision is still possible, and that by connecting with our higher selves and the natural world around us, we can create a more harmonious and sustainable society.

This idea has given rise to a variety of spiritual and environmental movements, including the eco-spirituality movement and the permaculture movement, which seek to create a more sustainable and equitable world by reconnecting with the natural world and living in harmony with the rhythms of the earth.

Finally, the legend of Atlantis has also been linked to the idea of a coming age of enlightenment, a time when humanity will reach a new level of spiritual and intellectual evolution. Many spiritual traditions and esoteric teachings predict that this age of enlightenment is just around the corner, and that it will be marked by a shift in consciousness and a new era of peace, harmony, and understanding.

While the specifics of this age of enlightenment vary widely between different traditions, many of them share the common themes of spiritual awakening, expanded consciousness, and the coming together of humanity in a new era of unity and harmony. This idea has given rise to a variety of new spiritual movements and practices, including New Age spirituality, which seeks to merge the best of traditional spiritual teachings with the latest scientific discoveries and cutting-edge metaphysical insights.

In conclusion, while the legend of Atlantis may be shrouded in mystery and speculation, its legacy can still be felt in contemporary times through the spiritual and metaphysical connections that it has inspired. From the quest for ancient wisdom and the pursuit of a lost utopia, to the promise of a new age of enlightenment and the coming together of humanity in a new era of unity and harmony, the legend of Atlantis continues to inspire and captivate people's imaginations to this day.

# Atlantis and Modern *POP*

The ancient city of Atlantis has captured the imagination of people for centuries, and contemporary pop alternative culture continues to show interest in this lost civilization. One significant example of this fascination is the song called "Atlantis" by Donovan, which was released in 1968. In this essay, we will explore the connection between the song and the contemporary pop alternative culture's continued interest in the ancient city, as well as what important history may have been lost in the flood.

Donovan's "Atlantis" is a psychedelic folk song that tells the story of a mythical land called Atlantis that sank beneath the waves. The song's lyrics are filled with references to ancient mythology, including the Greek god Zeus and the Egyptian god Osiris. Donovan sings about the beauty of Atlantis and the tragedy of its destruction, describing the city as a place of "crystal towers, great atlantis of the sea, with a crown of gold, a rose in its hair."

The song's popularity in the late 1960s coincided with a broader cultural interest in mythology, spirituality, and alternative forms of consciousness. This interest was fueled in part by the counterculture movement, which rejected mainstream values and sought to create a new, more liberated society. For many people, Atlantis represented a utopian ideal, a lost world of peace and harmony that could serve as a model for a new way of living.

Contemporary pop alternative culture continues to be fascinated by the story of Atlantis, and there are many possible reasons for this. One reason is that the story of Atlantis has become a symbol of humanity's hubris and the dangers of unchecked technological progress. According to the legend, Atlantis was a highly advanced civilization that became too arrogant and was punished by the gods with a catastrophic flood. This cautionary tale resonates with many people today, who worry about the negative consequences of rapid technological change and environmental degradation.

Another reason for the continued interest in Atlantis is the idea that the city may hold important secrets or knowledge that has been lost to history. Some people believe that the Atlanteans possessed advanced technology or spiritual wisdom that could be rediscovered and used to benefit humanity. This belief is part of a broader interest in ancient mysteries and alternative history, which has become increasingly popular in recent years.

However, it is important to acknowledge that the story of Atlantis is, at its core, a myth.

While there may be some historical basis for the legend, there is no concrete evidence that Atlantis ever existed as a real place. This means that any claims about the lost knowledge or technology of Atlantis must be treated with skepticism.

Moreover, the fascination with Atlantis can sometimes obscure the fact that there are many other ancient civilizations that have been lost to history, and whose stories are equally worthy of attention. The focus on Atlantis can sometimes lead to a Eurocentric perspective on history, in which the achievements of non-European cultures are overlooked or undervalued.

In conclusion, Donovan's "Atlantis" is a reflection of the cultural interest in the story of the lost city that has persisted for centuries. The song speaks to the idea of a utopian ideal, and the cautionary tale of unchecked technological progress. However, it is important to remember that the story of Atlantis is a myth, and any claims about lost knowledge or technology must be approached with skepticism. The fascination with Atlantis should not overshadow the equally compelling stories of other ancient civilizations that have been lost to history.

# What is the Fifth Dimension

The concept of living life in the fifth dimension is a complex and intriguing idea that has gained popularity in recent years. It suggests that there is a higher level of consciousness beyond the traditional physical realm that we exist in, and that by tapping into this dimension, we can elevate our experience of life and live in a state of greater harmony, peace, and joy.

To understand the concept of the fifth dimension, it's important to first understand the concept of dimensions themselves. In physics, dimensions refer to the measurable properties of an object or system, such as length, width, and height. However, in the context of spirituality and consciousness, dimensions refer to different levels of reality that exist beyond our physical realm.

The first dimension is the simplest and most basic level of existence, and refers to a single point in space. The second dimension adds length to this point, creating a line. The third dimension adds width, creating a plane, and the fourth dimension adds time, creating the space-time continuum that we currently exist in.

The fifth dimension, then, represents a higher level of existence beyond the physical realm. It is a state of being that transcends time and space, and is characterized by unity consciousness, love, and higher states of awareness. In the fifth dimension, there is a deep sense of interconnectedness and a recognition that all beings and things are part of the same universal consciousness.

Living life in the fifth dimension requires a shift in consciousness from the ego-based, fear-driven mindset of the third and fourth dimensions, to a mindset that is rooted in love, compassion, and unity. This shift can be challenging, as it requires letting go of old beliefs, patterns, and attachments that no longer serve us.

One way to begin the process of shifting into the fifth dimension is to practice mindfulness and meditation. By quieting the mind and turning inward, we can begin to connect with the higher aspects of our being and tap into the wisdom and guidance of our higher selves. Through meditation, we can also learn to cultivate a state of inner peace and calm, which is essential for living in the fifth dimension.

Another key aspect of living life in the fifth dimension is embracing a heart-centered approach to life. This means letting go of judgment, criticism, and negativity, and instead focusing on love, compassion, and understanding. When we approach life from a place of love and compassion, we are able to connect with others in a deeper way and experience greater levels of joy and fulfillment.

Living in the fifth dimension also requires a willingness to embrace change and to let go of the need for control. This can be challenging, as many of us are conditioned to seek security and stability in our lives. However, when we are able to let go of the need for control and surrender to the flow of life, we open ourselves up to new opportunities and experiences that can help us grow and evolve.

One of the most important aspects of living life in the fifth dimension is learning to trust the universe and the divine plan that is unfolding in our lives. This requires a deep faith and trust in the unseen forces that guide and support us, and a willingness to surrender to the greater wisdom of the universe.

Living in the fifth dimension is not a destination, but rather a continuous journey of growth, evolution, and self-discovery. It requires a commitment to ongoing personal development, and a willingness to let go of old beliefs and patterns that no longer serve us.

Ultimately, living life in the fifth dimension is about experiencing greater levels of joy, peace, and fulfillment in all areas of our lives. It is about embracing our true nature as spiritual beings, and recognizing that we are all part of the same interconnected web of life. By tapping into the higher consciousness of the fifth dimension, we can create a more harmonious, loving, and peaceful world for ourselves

# Living In the Fifth Dimension

The concept of living in the fifth dimension is often associated with spirituality and personal growth. It is a state of being where we are more aware of our true nature, and we live our lives from a place of love, compassion, and abundance. To live in the fifth dimension, we need to follow certain principles that can help us align with this state of consciousness. In this article, we will outline six core principles that can guide us in living our lives in the fifth dimension.

## 1. Practice Mindfulness and Awareness

Mindfulness and awareness are essential to living in the fifth dimension. This principle involves being present in the moment and paying attention to our thoughts, emotions, and surroundings. When we are mindful and aware, we can observe our thoughts and emotions without judgment and respond to situations in a more constructive way. We can also become more aware of our connection to the universe and the energy that flows through us. Mindfulness practices such as meditation, yoga, and breathing exercises can help us develop this skill.

### 2. Cultivate Gratitude

Gratitude is another essential principle for living in the fifth dimension. When we practice gratitude, we focus on the abundance in our lives rather than on what we lack. Gratitude helps us to recognize and appreciate the blessings in our lives, no matter how small they may seem. It also helps us to develop a positive mindset and attract more positivity into our lives. To cultivate gratitude, we can start by keeping a gratitude journal, focusing on the positive aspects of our lives, and expressing appreciation to those around us.

### 3. Live with Purpose

Living with purpose means aligning our actions and goals with our core values and beliefs. When we live with purpose, we have a clear direction in life and feel more fulfilled. This principle involves taking responsibility for our lives and making conscious choices that align with our goals and values. It also means being of service to others and contributing to the greater good. To live with purpose, we can start by identifying our values, setting meaningful goals, and taking action towards achieving them.

### 4. Practice Self-Love and Self-Care

Self-love and self-care are crucial principles

for living in the fifth dimension. When we love and care for ourselves, we create a foundation of self-worth and inner peace. Self-love involves accepting ourselves for who we are and embracing our strengths and weaknesses. Self-care involves taking care of our physical, emotional, and spiritual needs. It means prioritizing our well-being and creating healthy habits that nourish our body, mind, and soul. To practice self-love and self-care, we can start by setting healthy boundaries, engaging in activities that bring us joy, and taking time for rest and relaxation.

### 5. Embrace Unity and Oneness

Embracing unity and oneness is another key principle for living in the fifth dimension. This principle involves recognizing that we are all connected and part of a greater whole. When we embrace unity and oneness, we move beyond the limitations of our ego and see the world from a more expansive perspective. We also develop compassion and empathy for others and work towards creating a more harmonious world. To embrace unity and oneness, we can start by practicing forgiveness, embracing diversity, and recognizing the interconnectedness of all things.

### 6. Trust in the Universe

Trusting in the universe is the final principle for living in the fifth dimension. This principle involves having faith in the universe and trusting that everything happens for our highest good. When we trust in the universe, we let go of our need for control and surrender to the flow of life. We also develop a sense of inner peace and trust in our own intuition. To trust in the universe, we can start by practicing surrender, letting go of attachment, and trusting our intuition.

In conclusion, living in the fifth dimension requires a shift in consciousness and a willingness to embrace new ways of living. By following these six core principles, we can begin to align ourselves with this state of being and experience a more fulfilling and meaningful life. However, it's important to note that this is not a one-time effort, but rather a continuous journey of growth and evolution.

Living in the fifth dimension requires us to be mindful, grateful, purposeful, self-loving, unified, and trusting. It requires us to let go of our ego-based beliefs and embrace a more expansive perspective. It's about moving beyond fear and embracing love as the guiding force in our lives.

The journey towards living in the fifth dimension can be challenging at times, as it requires us to confront our limiting beliefs and patterns. However, the rewards are immeasurable, as we experience a sense of connection and harmony with ourselves, others, and the universe.

In addition to these core principles, it's important to remember that each person's journey towards the fifth dimension is unique. We all have our own lessons to learn and our own paths to follow. It's important to honor our individuality and trust that we are exactly where we need to be in our journey.

In conclusion, living in the fifth dimension is about living from a place of love, compassion, and abundance. By practicing mindfulness, gratitude, purpose, self-love, unity, and trust, we can begin to align ourselves with this state of being. It's a continuous journey of growth and evolution that requires us to let go of our limiting beliefs and patterns. With commitment and dedication, we can experience a more fulfilling and meaningful life, and contribute to creating a more harmonious world.

# *Poetic Recap*

*In the realms beyond our senses' grasp, Lies the fifth dimension, a wondrous clasp. A place of higher consciousness, a vibrant plane, Where the soul transcends, in a mystical gain.*

*Living in the fifth dimension, a cosmic state, Where love and light illuminate our fate. In this realm of unity, where all is one, We dance in harmony, beneath the sun.*
*In the fifth dimension, time flows anew, Past and future merge into a single view. The present moment, a timeless embrace, In this higher frequency, we find our grace.*

*Ego dissolves, and judgments fade away, In the fifth dimension, we choose to stay. It's a realm of pure potential, where dreams take flight, In the canvas of creation, we paint with light.*

*Living in the fifth dimension, we let love guide, As compassion and kindness, in our hearts reside. We connect with all beings, both near and far, In the fifth dimension, we're the shining star.*

*In this state of being, we manifest with ease, Our thoughts become reality, as we aim to please. With intention and love, we co-create our fate, In the fifth dimension, there's no need to wait.*

*But to live in this realm, we must open our heart, Let go of fear and ego, for a fresh start. In the fifth dimension, we transcend the strife, Embracing the oneness of all in life.*

*So, let us aspire to this higher plane, In the fifth dimension, where love shall reign. With open hearts and souls so bright, We'll elevate our world to a radiant height.*

*In the fifth dimension, we find our truth, A realm of abundance, where we're in our youth. Living in harmony, we become the light, In this cosmic dance, we take our flight.*

## What is Astrology

Astrology, a belief system and ancient practice that seeks to interpret the influence of celestial bodies on human affairs and natural phenomena, has captivated and intrigued civilizations for thousands of years. Rooted in the notion that the positions and movements of planets, stars, and other celestial entities can impact human lives and events on Earth, astrology has been both a source of guidance and a subject of controversy throughout history.

At the core of astrology lies the idea that there is a profound connection between the cosmos and human existence.

This connection is primarily expressed through the twelve zodiac signs, each associated with specific personality traits, characteristics, and life experiences. The zodiac is divided into four elements (fire, earth, air, and water) and three modalities (cardinal, fixed, and mutable), creating a dynamic framework that is believed to influence an individual's behaviors, preferences, and interactions.

The birth chart, often referred to as the natal chart or horoscope, is a central tool in astrology. It is a snapshot of the celestial positions at the exact moment of an individual's birth, including the positions of the Sun, Moon, and planets in relation to the twelve zodiac signs and the twelve houses. Astrologers analyze these elements to gain insights into a person's personality, relationships, career prospects, and life events.

Astrology is multifaceted, with different branches and systems that have evolved over time. Western astrology, also known as tropical astrology, is based on the position of the Sun relative to the Earth's equator and is the most popular form in many Western cultures. Vedic astrology, on the other hand, is rooted in ancient Indian traditions and is based on the sidereal zodiac, which considers the positions of celestial bodies in relation to fixed stars.

Critics of astrology often argue that its claims lack empirical evidence and scientific basis. Skeptics assert that the perceived connections between celestial events and human experiences are coincidental or psychologically driven, rather than indicative of any inherent cosmic influence. While the scientific community generally dismisses astrology as pseudoscience, its enduring popularity and cultural significance cannot be denied.

For many, astrology serves as a tool for self-discovery and introspection. Individuals turn to their horoscopes to gain insights into their strengths, weaknesses, and potential life paths. Astrology can provide a sense of reassurance and guidance, especially during times of uncertainty or important life transitions. Additionally, some people use astrology to navigate relationships, seeking compatibility insights through comparing birth charts.

The fascination with astrology has not waned with the advancement of modern science and technology. In fact, astrology has found a new home on the internet, with countless websites, apps, and social media accounts dedicated to providing horoscopes, compatibility analyses, and personalized astrological guidance. This digital resurgence has made astrology more accessible and relatable to younger generations, contributing to its continued popularity.

It's important to note that astrology is not a monolithic belief system. Interpretations and practices can vary widely among astrologers, and individuals may engage with astrology in diverse ways. Some see it as a fun and lighthearted hobby, while others deeply integrate astrological insights into their decision-making processes.

In conclusion, astrology remains a complex and enduring phenomenon that has captured human imagination for centuries. Its exploration of the relationship between celestial bodies and human life experiences has provided a unique lens through which people seek to understand themselves and their place in the universe. While astrology's scientific validity is widely disputed, its cultural significance, influence on art and literature, and role in personal introspection continue to make it a subject of fascination and contemplation for countless individuals around the world.

# *Poetic Recap*

*In the tapestry of the celestial night, Astrology unveils its timeless light. A language of stars, a cosmic rhyme, In the dance of the heavens, we mark our time.*

*Born from the union of Earth and sky, Astrology's wisdom, in our hearts does lie. The planets and stars, in their celestial quest, In the world of astrology, our lives are blessed.*

*From Aries to Pisces, the zodiac's call, Astrology's symbols, they enthrall us all. Each sign a story, a cosmic design, In the world of the stars, our destinies entwine.*

*The sun and the moon, in their sacred dance, Astrology reveals each soul's unique chance. To discover our purpose, our strengths, and our flaws, In the language of the stars, we find our cause.*

*With birth charts as maps, our lives unfold, Astrology's secrets, in its stories told. The houses and aspects, the planets' alignment, In the world of astrology, we seek enlightenment.*

*But astrology's magic is more than just fate, It's a mirror of soul, a cosmic estate. In the depths of our being, it helps us explore, In the language of the stars, we find even more.*

*The cycles of planets, the phases of the moon, Astrology's teachings, in its grand monsoon. A guide for the journey, as we navigate life, In the world of the stars, we conquer our strife.*

*So, let us embrace this celestial art, Astrology's wisdom, a treasure from the start. With open hearts and minds so wide, In the dance of the heavens, our spirits take flight.*

*In the grand cosmic tapestry, we find our place, Astrology's guidance, a gift of grace. With each star's twinkle, each planet's light, In the language of the stars, we discover our might.*

*In the realm of astrology, our souls unite, A celestial symphony, both day and night. With each birth chart cast, our stories align, In the world of the stars, our destinies entwine.*

## What is Astro-cartography

Astro-cartography, a fusion of astrology and cartography, offers a unique and intriguing perspective on how the positioning of celestial bodies can influence one's experiences and personal growth in different geographic locations. This practice suggests that the energies associated with specific planets and astrological aspects are somehow linked to particular regions on Earth, and by strategically planning travel or even relocating to these areas, individuals can enhance their well-being and spiritual development.

At the heart of astro-cartography lies the concept of "astrological lines" or "lines of influence." These lines are drawn on maps to indicate the paths of various planets, such as the Sun, Moon, and other significant celestial bodies, as they intersect with the Earth's surface. Depending on an individual's birth chart, certain planets may be considered more beneficial or auspicious for them, while others might be challenging or less supportive.

Advocates of astro-cartography argue that by identifying these lines and aligning oneself with the energies associated with them, one can tap into a deeper resonance with the universe and experience personal transformation. For instance, if a person's natal chart indicates a strong connection to the energy of Venus, spending time in a region where the Venus line runs might enhance their experiences related to love, relationships, and creativity.

Planning one's birthday around spending time in specific astro-cartographically significant areas is based on the idea that the energies present in those locations can profoundly influence the individual's upcoming year. Just as astrologers create solar return charts to analyze the astrological influences for the year ahead, astro-cartography suggests that certain places may provide more supportive and enriching environments for various aspects of one's life journey.

For example, if someone is looking to focus on personal growth and self-discovery in the coming year, they might consider spending their birthday in a location where the Sun line or other spiritually significant lines intersect. On the other hand, if career advancement is a priority, aligning with lines associated with Mercury or Jupiter could be beneficial.

It's important to note that astro-cartography is not universally accepted within the astrological community. Skeptics argue that the practice lacks empirical evidence and scientific validation. Critics suggest that any positive experiences individuals have in astrologically significant areas could be attributed to factors other than celestial energies, such as cultural immersion, personal mindset, or a simple change of environment.

However, proponents of astro-cartography contend that the practice is more about intention and connection than strict cause-and-effect relationships. They view it as a tool for deepening one's spiritual journey and exploring the interconnectedness between the cosmos and individual experiences.

In practice, astro-cartography involves a multi-step process. It begins with obtaining an accurate birth chart, which outlines the positions of celestial bodies at the time of an individual's birth. Then, an astrologer or individual uses specialized software to map out the lines of influence onto a world map. The next step is interpreting the lines in the context of the individual's birth chart and life goals.

Ultimately, whether one fully embraces astro-cartography or approaches it with curiosity, the practice offers a unique way to engage with astrology beyond traditional horoscopes.

It invites individuals to contemplate their relationship with the cosmos and explore the potential connections between celestial energies and their personal journey. Just as people travel to experience new cultures and landscapes, astro-cartography invites them to journey within, guided by the cosmic forces that have fascinated humans for millennia.

# *Poetic Recap*

*In the realm of astro-cartography, we chart a course, Through the cosmic tapestry, with a mystical force. A journey of discovery, guided by the stars' sway, In the maps of astrology, we find our way.*

*Astro-cartography, a celestial chart's grace, To explore the world, to find our place. With lines of destiny and points of light, In the atlas of stars, our dreams take flight.*

*Each longitude and latitude, a cosmic dance, In the world of astrology, we seize the chance. To align with the planets and their vibrant call, In astro-cartography, we discover it all.*

*The ascendant's direction, the midheaven's glow, In the maps of the cosmos, our destiny we show. With the moon's gentle guidance and the sun's warm embrace, In the language of stars, we find our own space.*

*Astro-cartography unveils a new horizon, A path of awareness, where the soul will widen. In the places we travel, in the cities we roam, In the world of astrology, we find our home.*

*With the nodal lines guiding our soul's intent, In the atlas of stars, our purpose is sent. To explore the energies, to embrace the unknown, In astro-cartography, our true selves are shown.*

*But remember, dear traveler, it's not all predestined, In the maps of the stars, free will is our lesson. To harness the energies, to follow our hearts, In the world of astrology, we play our parts.*

*So, let us embark on this cosmic voyage, In astro-cartography, with wisdom as our gauge. With open hearts and minds so wide, In the atlas of stars, our destinies ride.*

*In the grand design of life's grand parade, Astro-cartography, where dreams cascade. With each longitude and latitude, we're set to soar, In the world of astrology, forever wanting more.*

*As we navigate the heavens, our paths entwine, Astro-cartography, a celestial sign. With each star's twinkle, each planet's light, In the language of the stars, our futures ignite.*

## What is Numerology?

Numerology is often associated with signs and synchronicities, where specific numbers seem to repeatedly appear in one's life, carrying a deeper message or significance. These signs and synchronicities are believed to be messages from the universe, guiding individuals on their life path and offering insights into their journey. While skeptics may dismiss these occurrences as mere coincidences, numerology enthusiasts see them as meaningful and transformative experiences. Here are some examples of signs and synchronicities that numerology can help explain:

Repeating Numbers: One of the most common signs in numerology is encountering repeating numbers, such as 111, 222, 333, and so on. Each number holds a distinct vibration and meaning. For instance:

- 111: Often associated with new beginnings and alignment with your life purpose. It's a reminder to focus on your thoughts and intentions.

- 222: Represents harmony, balance, and cooperation. Encountering this number may signal that you are on the right track and that things are falling into place.

- 333: Symbolizes spiritual protection and guidance. It's a sign that your guardian angels are supporting you and guiding your path.

- 444: Indicates stability and a strong connection with the divine. It's a reminder that you are surrounded by love and protection.

- 555: Signifies change and transformation. Encountering this number may suggest that significant shifts are taking place in your life.

Birthdays and Important Dates: Numerology also places significance on birthdays and other important dates. Your Life Path Number, which is calculated from your birth date, provides insights into your core traits and life purpose. The numerological interpretation of your birth date can offer a deeper understanding of your strengths, challenges, and potential opportunities.

Name and Name Changes: Changing your name or encountering people with specific names can also carry numerological significance. Different names have different numerical values, and changing your name or encountering individuals with certain names can introduce new energies into your life. Some individuals choose to change their names based on numerological insights to align with their desired life path.

Address and Phone Numbers: The numerology of your address or phone number can also influence your experiences. Living or working at an address with specific numerical vibrations can affect your energy and interactions. Similarly, the digits in your phone number can carry messages or energies that resonate with your life's themes.

Synchronicities and Divine Timing: Numerology enthusiasts often experience synchronicities—meaningful coincidences that seem to be orchestrated by the universe. These synchronicities often involve numbers that align with an individual's life circumstances or choices. For example, encountering a specific number when you're contemplating a decision or facing a challenge can be seen as a sign that you're on the right path.

Personal Year Cycles: Numerology provides insights into personal year cycles, which offer guidance on the themes and energies that will be prominent in a given year. These cycles help individuals understand the overarching influences that will shape their experiences and decisions during that year. Knowing your personal year number can help you make informed choices and navigate challenges with greater awareness.

In essence, numerology suggests that numbers are not merely arbitrary symbols but carriers of profound meanings and energies. Signs and synchronicities involving numbers are thought to be messages from the universe, guiding individuals toward self-discovery, alignment with their life purpose, and a deeper connection with the cosmos. While interpretations of these signs may vary among numerologists, many people find comfort and empowerment in recognizing and interpreting the numerical patterns that manifest in their lives. Whether viewed as cosmic guidance or a product of the subconscious mind, the study of numerology offers a fascinating perspective on the interconnectedness of numbers and human experience.

The numerology of your name and date of birth holds a wealth of insights and symbolism that can provide a deeper understanding of your personality, life path, and potential life experiences. By exploring the numerical vibrations associated with your name and birth date, you can uncover hidden patterns, strengths, challenges, and opportunities that shape your journey through life.

Numerology of Your Name: Your name, as a combination of letters, carries specific numerical values based on the alphabet. Each letter is assigned a numerical value, often following the Pythagorean or Chaldean system. By adding the values of the letters in your name and reducing them to a single digit (or a master number, if applicable), you can calculate your Expression Number or Destiny Number. This number reflects your core traits, abilities, and potential life path.

For example, if your name is "John Smith," the numerical values for each letter would be: J=1, O=6, H=8, N=5, S=1, M=4, I=9, T=2, H=8. Adding these values (1 + 6 + 8 + 5 + 1 + 4 + 9 + 2 + 8) equals 44. Since 44 is a master number, you would not reduce it further. In this case, your Destiny Number would be 44.

Your Expression Number offers insights into your natural talents, strengths, and how you express yourself in the world. It can provide clarity on your career path, creative abilities, and how you communicate with others. A master number in your Expression Number indicates that you possess a strong and impactful energy, often associated with leadership and a higher sense of purpose.

Numerology of Your Birth Date: Your birth date carries significant numerical vibrations that can be interpreted using numerology. The most important number derived from your birth date is your Life Path Number. To calculate this number, add the digits of your birth date (day, month, and year) and reduce them to a single digit (or a master number, if applicable). Your Life Path Number reflects your life purpose, challenges, and opportunities.

For instance, if you were born on March 15, 1985, the calculation would be: 3 (March) + 15 + 1985 = 2003. Then, 2 + 0 + 0 + 3 = 5. In this case, your Life Path Number would be 5.

Your Life Path Number offers insights into your innate tendencies, life journey, and lessons you are meant to learn. It can shed light on your strengths, weaknesses, and how you navigate different aspects of your life. For example, a Life Path Number of 5 suggests a path characterized by freedom, adventure, and change. Individuals with this number may excel in careers that involve travel, communication, and versatility.

Interpreting the Combined Numerology: When you combine the numerology of your name and birth date, you gain a more comprehensive understanding of yourself. Your Expression Number and Life Path Number interact to shape your personality traits, life experiences, and potential outcomes. For instance, if your Expression Number indicates strong leadership qualities (such as the master number 44), and your Life Path Number is 1 (the number of independence and new beginnings), you may be destined to lead and initiate transformative changes.

Furthermore, exploring the interactions between your name and birth date can reveal hidden patterns and connections. Certain numbers may appear more frequently in your name or birth date, highlighting specific areas of emphasis in your life. For example, if the number 7 is prominent in both your name and birth date, it may signify a strong inclination towards spirituality, introspection, and a quest for deeper knowledge.

In conclusion, the numerology of your name and date of birth offers a fascinating and insightful journey into your unique qualities, life purpose, and potential experiences. By delving into the vibrations of numbers and their meanings, you can gain a deeper awareness of your strengths, challenges, and opportunities. Numerology serves as a valuable tool for self-discovery, providing a framework to understand your true essence and navigate your life's path with greater insight and purpose.

# *Poetic Recap*

*In the language of numbers, a secret code, Numerology unveils the path we're bestowed. A mystical science, where meanings entwine, In the dance of the digits, our destinies align.*

*From one to nine, each number holds sway, Numerology's wisdom, in its unique way. Each number a symbol, a story to tell, In the world of numerology, we decipher well.*

*Number one, a symbol of new beginnings, In the realm of ambition, its energy's spinning. With leadership and courage, it lights the way, In numerology's tapestry, we find our say.*

*Number two, the harmonizer's embrace, In partnerships and balance, it finds its space. With empathy and love, it seeks to connect, In the language of numbers, our souls intersect. Number three, a trinity of creativity and fun, In the world of expression, it's second to none. With joy and enthusiasm, it leads the dance, In numerology's realm, we take a chance.*

*Number four, a symbol of stability and base, In the structure of life, it finds its place. With diligence and order, it builds the ground, In the dance of numbers, we're firmly bound.*

*Number five, the wanderer's call, In the realm of adventure, it stands tall. With freedom and change, it breaks the mold, In numerology's story, our spirits are bold.*

*Number six, a symbol of love's embrace, In family and home, it finds its grace. With nurturing and care, it guides the heart, In the world of numbers, we're never apart.*

*Number seven, the seeker's quest, In the realm of*

*wisdom, it's put to the test. With intuition and introspection, it seeks to find, In numerology's journey, the soul's design.*

*Number eight, the achiever's might, In abundance and power, it takes flight. With determination and vision, it paves the way, In the language of numbers, we seize the day.*

*Number nine, a symbol of endings and renewal, In the world of completion, it's the soul's fuel. With compassion and selflessness, it takes its stand, In numerology's wisdom, we understand.*

*So, let us delve into this mystical art, Numerology's secrets, where meanings impart. With open minds and hearts so free, In the dance of numbers, our destinies we'll see.*

*In the tapestry of life's grand parade, Numerology's guidance, where dreams cascade. With each number's essence, with each digit's light, In the language of numbers, we find our insight.*

# GAIA THEORY

The Gaia principle, also known as Gaia theory or Gaia hypothesis, is a scientific concept that suggests that the Earth is a self-regulating system that maintains a state of balance and stability necessary for the continuation of life on the planet. This idea was first proposed in the 1970s by British scientist James Lovelock and American biologist Lynn Margulis. The name "Gaia" comes from the ancient Greek goddess of the Earth.

The central idea behind the Gaia principle is that the Earth's biosphere, atmosphere, oceans, and geology work together to create and maintain conditions suitable for life. This is accomplished through a complex system of feedback loops and interactions that regulate the planet's temperature, composition, and other factors. For example, the Earth's atmosphere is rich in oxygen, which is produced by photosynthetic organisms such as plants and algae. This oxygen, in turn, supports the respiratory systems of animals, including humans.

The Gaia principle suggests that the Earth is not just a passive container for life but an active participant in its own evolution. The Earth's living and non-living components are interdependent and influence each other in complex ways. The Gaia hypothesis proposes that the Earth's biosphere acts like a giant organism, with feedback loops and regulatory mechanisms that maintain the stability of the system.

One of the most important concepts in the Gaia principle is the notion of homeostasis. Homeostasis is the ability of a system to maintain a relatively stable internal environment, despite changes in external conditions. In the context of the Earth, this means that the planet's living and non-living components work together to regulate the temperature, atmospheric composition, and other factors necessary for life to exist. For example, when the Earth's temperature rises, the oceans absorb more carbon dioxide, which helps to cool the planet. This feedback loop helps to maintain a stable climate.

Another important aspect of the Gaia principle is the role of feedback loops in the Earth's system. Feedback loops are mechanisms that allow a system to respond to changes in its environment. There are two types of feedback loops: positive feedback loops and negative feedback loops. Positive feedback loops amplify changes, while negative feedback loops dampen them. In the context of the Earth, both types of feedback loops are important in maintaining the planet's stability.

Critics of the Gaia principle argue that it is overly anthropomorphic, meaning that it assigns human-like qualities to non-human entities such as the Earth. They also contend that the Gaia hypothesis is not testable or falsifiable, and therefore does not meet the criteria for a scientific theory. However, proponents of the Gaia principle argue that it is a useful framework for understanding the complex interactions between the Earth's living and non-living components.

Despite the controversy surrounding the Gaia principle, it has had a significant impact on the fields of ecology and environmental science. The concept of homeostasis and the importance of feedback loops have become central ideas in these fields. The Gaia principle has also inspired a new generation of scientists and environmentalists who are committed to understanding and protecting the Earth's ecosystems.

In conclusion, the Gaia principle is a scientific concept that suggests that the Earth is a self-regulating system that maintains a state of balance and stability necessary for the continuation of life on the planet. While the idea has its critics, it has had a significant impact on our understanding of the Earth's ecosystems and has inspired a new generation of scientists and environmentalists.

## *Poetic Recap*

*In the heart of Earth's embrace, a theory takes flight, The Gaia Theory, a vision so bright. A notion that Earth is a living, breathing being, In the web of life, we find its meaning.*

*From the depths of oceans to the mountain's high peak, Gaia's heartbeat pulses, in the ecosystems we seek. A complex synergy, a harmonious dance, In the Gaia Theory, we find our chance. Every forest, every river, every creature that crawls, Gaia's presence surrounds us, in her nurturing thralls. From the microscopic to the grand and immense, In the world of Gaia, there's no room for pretense.*

*She regulates temperature, keeps balance in check, In the Gaia Theory, we find deep respect. A self-regulating system, so ancient and wise, In the web of Gaia, our existence relies.*

*Yet, in our heedless ways, we've caused her dismay, Disrupting the balance, leading life astray. In the Gaia Theory, a lesson we learn, To care for our Earth, for which we should yearn.*

*In the tapestry of life, Gaia's threads are entwined, In the Gaia Theory, we see the design. A call to protect her, to cherish and mend, In the world of Gaia, our love must extend.*

*With each tree that's planted, each river restored, In the Gaia Theory, our commitment is stored. To honor her essence, in every step we take, In the embrace of Gaia, our future's at stake.*

*So, let us heed this theory, this wisdom so grand, The Gaia Theory, a truth for the land. With love and devotion, let our actions align, In the world of Gaia, our destinies entwine.*

*In the grand symphony of life's endless song, The Gaia Theory, where we all belong. With reverence and care, may our voices unite, In the language of Gaia, let us shine our light.*

# THE GOLDEN RATIO

The Golden Ratio, also known as the Divine Proportion or Phi (⊠), is a mathematical concept that has fascinated mathematicians, artists, and scientists for centuries. It is a number that has been observed in various natural and man-made phenomena, and it is believed to possess aesthetic and harmonious qualities. The Golden Ratio is approximately equal to 1.6180339887, and it has a profound influence on art, architecture, nature, and even the human body.

The Golden Ratio can be mathematically defined as follows: if a line is divided into two parts such that the ratio of the whole line to the longer part is equal to the ratio of the longer part to the shorter part, then this ratio is equal to the Golden Ratio. Symbolically, this can be expressed as $(a + b) / a = a / b = \varphi$.

One of the earliest known appearances of the Golden Ratio dates back to ancient Greece, where it was discovered and studied by mathematicians like Euclid and Pythagoras. It was considered a fundamental concept in geometry and was often associated with beauty and harmony. In fact, the Golden Ratio was believed to be the key to aesthetically pleasing proportions and was used extensively in Greek architecture and art.

The Golden Ratio can be found in numerous examples of natural phenomena. It is seen in the spiral patterns of seashells, the branching of trees, and the arrangement of leaves and petals in flowers. For instance, the spirals of a nautilus shell or a sunflower often exhibit a consistent expansion based on the Golden Ratio. These natural occurrences suggest that the Golden Ratio plays a role in the growth and development of living organisms.

The human body is also said to exhibit proportions based on the Golden Ratio. It is believed that certain body measurements, such as the ratio of the height of the navel to the total height, the ratio of the length of the forearm to the hand, and the ratio of the length of the face to the width, approximate the Golden Ratio. These proportions are thought to contribute to the perception of beauty and attractiveness.

Artists and architects throughout history have been inspired by the Golden Ratio and have incorporated it into their works. Renaissance painters, such as Leonardo da Vinci, used the Golden Ratio to establish balanced and visually appealing compositions in their artwork. Architects, like Le Corbusier and Frank Lloyd Wright, applied the Golden Ratio in their designs, believing that it enhanced the aesthetic appeal and harmony of their buildings.

The influence of the Golden Ratio extends beyond the realm of visual arts. It has also been observed in music, with composers utilizing the ratio in the construction of melodies and harmonies. The division of a musical composition into sections, such as the length of movements in a symphony or the proportions of a musical phrase, can follow the principles of the Golden Ratio.

The fascination with the Golden Ratio is not limited to its aesthetic and artistic applications. It has also found its way into fields such as mathematics, computer science, and even stock market analysis. The Fibonacci sequence, a series of numbers in which each number is the sum of the two preceding ones (starting with 0 and 1), is closely related to the Golden Ratio. This sequence appears in many natural phenomena and has practical applications in fields such as computer algorithms and data analysis.

While the exact influence and significance of the Golden Ratio are still debated among scholars, its ubiquity in nature and its recurring appearance in human creations cannot be denied. Whether it is a reflection of an underlying universal principle of beauty and harmony or a coincidence of mathematics and aesthetics, the Golden Ratio continues to captivate our imagination and inspire our creative endeavors. Its allure lies in its ability to bridge the gap between mathematics and art, providing a fascinating glimpse into the interconnectedness of the natural world and the human mind.

# *Poetic Recap*

*In the world of numbers, a divine refrain, Resides the Golden Ratio, a mystical terrain. A mathematical masterpiece, a sacred proportion, In its elegant harmony, we find our devotion.*

*From ancient Greece to nature's grand design, The Golden Ratio's presence, forever divine. A spiral of beauty, a pattern so true, In the dance of numbers, we find our cue.*

*A number, approximately 1.618, In its perfect symmetry, we celebrate. The ratio of a line divided just right, In the world of mathematics, it takes its flight.*

*In art and architecture, it takes its place, The Golden Ratio's grace, we can't efface. From the*

*Parthenon's columns to Da Vinci's art, In the language of proportions, it's a work of heart. But the Golden Ratio's magic is more than just math, It's a symbol of beauty, on a different path. In the swirl of seashells, in the petals of a rose, In the wonders of nature, its presence it shows.*

*From galaxies in space to the flowers on Earth, The Golden Ratio's magic, from birth to birth. A spiral of life, a pattern so clear, In the world of creation, it's ever near.*

*In the human form, it's found once more, From fingertips to navel, as we explore. A blueprint of nature, in each of us resides, In the dance of the Golden Ratio, our essence abides.*

*So, let us honor this proportion divine, The Golden Ratio's wisdom, in every line. With open minds and hearts aligned, In the world of numbers, our souls entwined.*

*In the grand mosaic of life's endless quest, The Golden Ratio, where beauty finds its nest. With every spiral and proportion's decree, In the language of numbers, we find harmony.*

# THE INTERCONNECTEDNESS OF ALL THINGS

The idea that everything is a reflection of everything else is a profound and intriguing concept that has been explored by many cultures and spiritual traditions throughout human history. This idea suggests that the world we experience is not separate from ourselves but is intimately connected to us in a way that we often fail to recognize. It implies that the things we perceive in the world are not just random occurrences, but rather are reflections of our own thoughts, beliefs, and emotions.

Nature is perhaps the most obvious example of this idea. When we observe the natural world, we see a vast array of different forms and phenomena, from the smallest insects to the largest mountains. Each of these elements is interconnected and interdependent, and together they form a complex web of life. The cycles of the seasons, the patterns of the weather, and the movements of the stars and planets are all part of this interconnected system.

Moreover, we can see that the natural world often mirrors the qualities and characteristics of human beings. For example, we might observe how a powerful storm or a raging wildfire can mirror the intensity of our own emotions, or how the calm stillness of a mountain lake can reflect our own inner peace. We might also notice how the intricate patterns of a flower or the delicate balance of a bird's wings can mirror our own sense of beauty and harmony.

But it's not just the natural world that is a reflection of ourselves. The objects and people around us are also part of this mirror reflection.

When we interact with others, we are often drawn to people who share similar values, interests, and beliefs. Likewise, we might notice that the people who challenge us or irritate us are often reflecting back aspects of ourselves that we find difficult to accept or acknowledge.

This idea can be both empowering and challenging. On the one hand, it suggests that we have the power to shape our world by changing our own thoughts, beliefs, and emotions. If we want to see more beauty, harmony, and peace in the world, we can cultivate those qualities within ourselves and watch as they are reflected back to us. On the other hand, it also means that we cannot escape the parts of ourselves that we find difficult or uncomfortable. The world will continue to mirror back those parts until we are ready to confront and transform them.

One way to explore this idea in more depth

is through the practice of mindfulness. By cultivating a non-judgmental awareness of our thoughts, emotions, and sensations, we can begin to see how they are reflected in the world around us. We might notice, for example, how our mood affects our perception of the world, or how the things we focus on tend to become more prominent in our experience.

Another way to explore this idea is through the practice of gratitude. By focusing on the things we appreciate and value in our lives, we can begin to see how they are reflected back to us. We might notice, for example, how expressing gratitude for the people in our lives tends to strengthen those relationships, or how appreciating the beauty of nature tends to deepen our connection to the natural world.

In conclusion, the idea that everything is a reflection of everything else is a fascinating and thought-provoking concept that invites us to look more deeply into our own experience of the world. By recognizing the interconnectedness of all things, we can begin to see how our thoughts, emotions, and beliefs shape our reality. We can also begin to cultivate a deeper sense of appreciation and gratitude for the world around us, knowing that it is a mirror reflection of our own inner landscape.

## *Poetic Recap*

*In the grand tapestry of existence, we find, The interconnectedness of all things, a truth defined. A web of life, where threads intertwine, In this cosmic dance, our destinies align.*

*From the depths of the ocean to the heights of the sky, The interconnectedness of all things, we can't deny. Every leaf, every rock, every creature that springs, In the world of connection, our heartstrings sing.*

*The butterfly's flutter, the storm's raging gale, In the interconnectedness of all things, we set sail. A ripple in water, a whispering breeze, In the language of nature, we find our ease.*

*In the hearts of strangers, in the touch of a friend, The interconnectedness of all things, we comprehend. Every smile, every tear, every love that abounds, In the realm of emotions, our unity resounds.*

*From the stars in the cosmos to the Earth's fertile ground, The interconnectedness of all things, it does astound. Each atom, each molecule, in its intricate dance, In the world of science, we find our chance.*

*But it's more than just science, it's a spiritual quest, The interconnectedness of all things, in our hearts does rest. In the wisdom of sages, in ancient lore, In the language of the soul, we explore more.*

*In the cycle of life, from birth to decay, The interconnectedness of all things, in every way. A circle unbroken, a cycle complete, In the tapestry of existence, we're all but a beat.*

*So, let us honor this truth, let it guide our stride, The interconnectedness of all things, in life's grand tide. With open hearts and minds, let us embrace, In the world of connection, find our sacred space.*

*In the grand symphony of life's endless song, The interconnectedness of all things, where we all belong. With every breath we take, every soul that sings, In the language of love, our oneness springs.*

# MODERN VOICES RUNNING THE PROGRAM THAT IS THE 3 6 9 METHOD

Abraham Hicks is the name given to a group of non-physical entities that are channeled through Esther Hicks. Esther Hicks and her husband Jerry Hicks were the first to receive and share the teachings of Abraham Hicks, and since Jerry's passing, Esther has continued to share their message with the world.

Abraham Hicks teachings center around the idea that we are all vibrational beings, and that we have the power to create our reality through our thoughts and emotions. The basic premise of their message is that we are all connected to a universal consciousness, and that we can tap into this consciousness to create the life we desire.

Abraham Hicks teaches that the law of attraction is a powerful force that can be used to create the life we want. The law of attraction is the idea that we attract what we focus on, whether positive or negative. By focusing on positive thoughts and emotions, we can attract positive experiences into our lives.

Abraham Hicks also teaches that our emotions are our guidance system, and that we should follow our emotions to find our true path in life. They believe that when we are in alignment with our true selves, we will feel joy, love, and abundance.

So how can one find and connect with the teachings of Abraham Hicks? The first step is to become familiar with their message. There are many books, videos, and online resources available that can help you learn more about their teachings. Once you have a basic understanding of their message, you can begin to practice their teachings in your own life.

One way to practice the teachings of Abraham Hicks is to focus on positive thoughts and emotions. This can be done through daily affirmations, visualization exercises, or simply by focusing on things that bring you joy and happiness.

Another way to connect with the teachings of Abraham Hicks is to attend one of their workshops or seminars. These events are held all over the world, and offer the opportunity to learn directly from Esther Hicks and the non-physical entities that she channels.

Finally, it is important to remember that connecting with the teachings of Abraham Hicks is a personal journey. What works for one person may not work for another, so it is important to stay open and flexible in your approach.

So why is what Abraham Hicks is doing through channeling in alignment with the spiritual laws and principles of the universe and the law of attraction? The answer lies in their message of oneness and the power of positive thinking.

Abraham Hicks teaches that we are all connected to a universal consciousness, and that we can tap into this consciousness to create the life we desire. This message is in line with many spiritual traditions, which teach that we are all connected and that our thoughts and actions have an impact on the world around us.

The law of attraction is also a central part of Abraham Hicks teachings. This law is based on the idea that we attract what we focus on, whether positive or negative. By focusing on positive thoughts and emotions, we can attract positive experiences into our lives.

Finally, the message of Abraham Hicks is rooted in the principle of love and compassion. They teach that we should follow our emotions to find our true path in life, and that when we are in alignment with our true selves, we will feel joy, love, and abundance.

In conclusion, Abraham Hicks and Esther Hicks have shared a powerful message of oneness, positivity, and the law of attraction with the world. Their teachings have helped countless people to create the life they desire, and to find joy and abundance in their lives. By connecting with their teachings, we can tap into the power of the universe and create a life filled with love and abundance.

# Closing thoughts... Signs and synchronicities & conscious remembering

There is an infinite point and space in every room. Even a room without a view. There is always an orientation toward a greater opening. An emerging and expanding focus. A divine pulse and creativity. Life is constantly giving us energetic puzzles to solve. As we awaken and rise, we learn to raise our frequencies to resolve and reduce any outstanding particles waiting to be embraced and aligned. We are all always learning to love. To open, to stay open, and to create space for healing, in all places and at all times. This is the unfolding mystery of the divine.

# A WalknTalk down memory lane…

In 2012 I created my first brand around the concept of living in flow. It was called WalknTalk. I was making leather notebooks and had first begun doing so in Argentina in 2010. Inspired to bring a message to the world about transforming your life with a trip and "Getting Lost to Find Yourself", I believed that the most important thing I could do with my life was to carry forth this message. I believed that my transformation that happened in 2007-2008 as an exchange student was so extraordinary that I had to discover more about the metaphysics behind my change.

The logo that emerged from the WalknTalk brand was later articulated in an infographic in which I depicted the meaning of the various lines. It was through this depiction that I realized the crux of finding and living in flow.

It was as if the symbol spoke to me. It said Ground Yourself, Propel Through Purpose, Expand into Flow.

I make a poster about it and in December of 2014 I printed a 24 x 36 inch declaration to Get Lost To Find Yourself. I sat at Javas Coffee in downtown Rochester, New York and invited all of my friends, fans, and family to come sign it. It was that January that I embarked on a journey throughout eastern europe and then ending in Portugal. I thought I was going to spend 5 days in Portugal, but instead I missed four flights and stayed for forty-five days.

My desire to live there continued manifesting over the next 5 years, and in 2020 it finally happened. All of my entrepreneurial skills culminated in a venture that quickly gave me the funds I needed during the pandemic, and

I made the massive move in one huge leap of faith. I currently have homes in Portugal and Brasil, and live a life of total flow and freedom.

People sometimes ask how I did it all so quickly. The truth is, I already had the clear picture. I was propelling through purpose, expanding into flow, and continued to ground myself along the way.

The universe loves to expand through us, and when we lean into what's uncomfortable, and trust with all of our being, success in the future is not a question but a certainty.

Building our mindset like a kiln burning with a yearning burning desire and a clear picture of what we want is a sure way to manifest it.

# People in History Who Knew This

Martin Luther King
Darkness cannot drive out darkness, only light can do that.

Martin Luther King Jr. was a towering figure in the civil rights movement of the 1950s and 1960s. His unwavering belief in equality, justice, and nonviolent resistance transformed the course of history and continues to inspire people around the world. King's remarkable achievements and enduring legacy are a testament to the power of believing in a cause greater than oneself.

King's belief in the inherent worth and equality of every individual was the driving force behind his advocacy for civil rights. He envisioned a society where individuals would be judged not by the color of their skin but by the content of their character. His powerful speeches, such as the iconic "I Have a Dream" speech delivered during the March on Washington in 1963, resonated deeply with people across racial, ethnic, and social divides. His ability to articulate a vision of a just and inclusive society fueled the hope and determination of millions.

King's unwavering commitment to nonviolent resistance was deeply rooted in his belief in the power of love and forgiveness. He drew inspiration from the teachings of Mahatma Gandhi and applied them to the struggle for racial equality in the United States. Despite facing violent opposition, King remained steadfast in his conviction that love and nonviolence were powerful tools for social change. His adherence to these principles allowed him to unite people, transcend hatred, and expose the injustice and inequality that plagued society.

King's belief in the power of believing extended beyond his own personal convictions. He had an extraordinary ability to instill hope and inspire action in others. Through his leadership and impassioned speeches, he rallied countless individuals to join the civil rights movement and actively work towards a more just and equal society. He believed that when people unite around a shared vision and work together, they can bring about transformative change.

Martin Luther King Jr.'s impact and legacy are a testament to the transformative power of believing. His unwavering belief in equality, justice, and nonviolent resistance served as a catalyst for change, challenging the status quo and inspiring others to do the same. His vision, courage, and dedication continue to remind us that belief in a better world and the power of collective action can overcome even the most entrenched social injustices. As we reflect on his life and teachings, we are reminded that our beliefs shape our actions and have the potential to shape the world around us.

Goethe
Be Bold and Mighty Forces will Come to You

Johann Wolfgang von Goethe, the German literary genius of the 18th and 19th centuries, is known for his influential works and his profound impact on literature, philosophy, and the arts. Among his many notable quotes, one that stands out is "Be bold and mighty forces will come to your aid." This powerful statement encapsulates Goethe's belief in the transformative power of courage, initiative, and daring.

Goethe himself lived by this principle, taking risks and pushing boundaries throughout his life. He explored a wide range of artistic disciplines, including poetry, drama, novels, and scientific writing, demonstrating his relentless curiosity and creative spirit. His most renowned work, "Faust," captures the essence of his philosophy, delving into the depths of the human condition and the pursuit of knowledge and fulfillment.

"Be bold and mighty forces will come to your aid" encourages individuals to step out of their comfort zones, confront challenges, and embrace opportunities. Goethe believed that when one displays courage and takes decisive action, the universe responds by providing support, resources, and unforeseen opportunities. This philosophy resonates with the idea that a proactive and determined approach can attract positive outcomes and open doors that would have otherwise remained closed.

The essence of Goethe's quote lies in its recognition of the interconnectedness between personal initiative and external forces. By summoning the courage to pursue our dreams and aspirations, we set in motion a chain of events that can lead to unexpected assistance, synchronicities, and favorable circumstances. It is a call to action, urging individuals to overcome their fears, doubts, and limitations and embrace the limitless potential within them.

This principle can be applied to various aspects of life, including personal growth, professional pursuits, and creative endeavors. It encourages individuals to think big, take calculated risks, and have the audacity to pursue their passions. It reminds us that we are not mere spectators in our own lives but active participants who have the power to shape our destinies.

Goethe's timeless wisdom continues to inspire and motivate individuals to this day. It serves as a reminder that our willingness to be bold and embrace challenges can unlock our full potential and attract the support and opportunities needed to achieve our goals. By embodying courage, determination, and audacity, we tap into the mighty forces of the universe and set ourselves on a path of growth, fulfillment, and extraordinary achievement.

# Winston Churchill

Never, never, never give up.

Winston Churchill, the iconic British statesman and leader, is regarded as one of the most influential figures of the 20th century. His indomitable spirit, unwavering resolve, and powerful oratory skills made him a symbol of courage and leadership, particularly during the tumultuous years of World War II. Churchill's legacy as a wartime Prime Minister and his contributions to history continue to inspire generations.

Churchill's leadership during World War II is particularly notable. As Prime Minister of the United Kingdom from 1940 to 1945, he rallied the British people and inspired them to withstand the relentless onslaught of Nazi Germany. His resolute determination and refusal to surrender in the face of overwhelming odds became emblematic of the British spirit and defiance.

Churchill's speeches, such as the famous "We Shall Fight on the Beaches" address, galvanized the nation and provided hope during some of the darkest days of the war. His powerful words, delivered with passion and conviction, instilled a sense of purpose and unity, reminding the British people that victory was possible even in the face of adversity.

Beyond his wartime leadership, Churchill had a long and varied career in politics and public service. He served as a Member of Parliament, held various government positions, and was Prime Minister for two separate terms. Churchill was known for his astute political judgment, strategic thinking, and determination to defend the principles of freedom and democracy.

Churchill was also a prolific writer, receiving the Nobel Prize in Literature in 1953 for his historical and biographical works. His writings, including his memoirs, provide invaluable insights into the events and decisions that shaped the 20th century.

Churchill's impact extends beyond his political and literary achievements. He personified resilience, tenacity, and the ability to lead in times of crisis. His unwavering belief in the power of democracy, freedom, and human dignity continues to resonate and inspire leaders around the world.

Winston Churchill's legacy remains enduring, a testament to the strength of character, leadership, and determination. His words and actions during some of humanity's most challenging times exemplify the qualities necessary to overcome adversity and make a lasting impact. Churchill's contribution to history serves as a reminder of the importance of courage, conviction, and unwavering dedication to the ideals that define us as a society. His leadership, both on the battlefield and in the political arena, continues to inspire leaders and individuals to strive for greatness, never backing down in the pursuit of a better future.

Bob Proctor
You are the only problem you will ever have and you are the only solution.

Bob Proctor is a renowned personal development coach, author, and speaker who has made a significant impact on the field of self-improvement. Throughout his career, Proctor has emphasized the principles of deduction and the transformative power of ideas and images in shaping one's existence.

Deduction, as Proctor teaches, involves the process of reasoning and drawing logical conclusions based on available information. It is about analyzing and discerning the underlying causes and effects in our lives. Proctor encourages individuals to apply deductive reasoning to their thoughts, beliefs, and actions, in order to uncover the root causes of their circumstances and make necessary changes.

Proctor firmly believes that our thoughts and beliefs shape our reality. He emphasizes the importance of cultivating a positive mindset and adopting empowering beliefs.

According to his teachings, our thoughts create images in our mind, which in turn generate corresponding emotions and influence our actions. By consciously directing our thoughts and consistently focusing on positive mental images, we can attract the desired outcomes into our lives.

Proctor emphasizes the power of ideas and images in molding and shaping our existence. He teaches that everything in our external reality begins as an idea or image in our minds. By consistently holding positive and empowering ideas, we can set in motion a creative process that manifests those ideas into physical reality.

To effectively shape our existence through ideas and images, Proctor emphasizes the importance of clarity, focus, and persistence. He encourages individuals to set clear and specific goals, vividly visualize the desired outcomes, and consistently reinforce those images through affirmations and actions.

Proctor's teachings align with the principles of the law of attraction and the power of visualization, which have gained recognition in the field of personal development. His emphasis on the conscious shaping of thoughts, beliefs, and mental images resonates with the idea that our internal world creates our external reality.

Bob Proctor's work serves as a reminder that our thoughts and beliefs have the power to shape our existence. By applying the principles of deduction, consciously directing our thoughts, and consistently holding positive mental images, we can manifest the outcomes we desire. His teachings provide a roadmap for personal growth, encouraging individuals to take control of their thoughts and actively create the life they envision.

James Allen
You are today where your thoughts have brought you; you will be tomorrow where your thoughts take you.

James Allen was a British philosophical writer and poet who lived from 1864 to 1912. He is best known for his inspirational and self-help writings, particularly his book "As a Man Thinketh." The quote you mentioned, "Our mind is like a garden, anything planted in it will surely grow," is often attributed to him.

In "As a Man Thinketh," Allen explores the power of our thoughts and their impact on our lives. He presents the idea that our minds are like fertile gardens, and our thoughts are the seeds we plant within them. Just as a well-tended garden produces beautiful flowers and bountiful fruits, the thoughts we cultivate in our minds manifest in our actions and shape our reality.

Allen emphasizes the importance of personal responsibility and self-awareness. He suggests that by consciously choosing positive and constructive thoughts, we can create a mental environment that nurtures growth, happiness, and success. Conversely, negative and limiting thoughts will yield undesirable outcomes and hinder our progress.

The analogy of the mind as a garden serves as a reminder that we have control over our thoughts, attitudes, and beliefs. We can weed out negative thinking patterns and cultivate positive ones through mindfulness, self-reflection, and consistent effort. By planting seeds of gratitude, optimism, and self-belief, we create the conditions for personal transformation and fulfillment.

James Allen's teachings continue to resonate with readers worldwide. His profound insights into the power of the mind have inspired countless individuals to take charge of their thoughts and ultimately shape their lives. The notion that our minds are like gardens provides a simple yet profound metaphor for understanding the influence of our thoughts and the potential for growth and self-improvement.

Through James Allen's timeless wisdom, we are reminded that our thoughts are potent forces that shape our reality. By sowing positive and empowering thoughts, we can cultivate a life filled with abundance, joy, and fulfillment.

Wallace Wattles
By thought, the thing you want is brought to you. By action, you receive it.

Wallace Wattles, an influential writer and pioneer of the New Thought movement, is best known for his book "The Science of Getting Rich." In this transformative work, he explores the power of thought and the concept that all things in the universe are created from a universal substance.

The quote you mentioned, "There is a thinking stuff from which all things are made that in its essence permeates and penetrates all corners of the world," encapsulates one of the core ideas put forth by Wattles. He posits that there is a fundamental substance or energy that underlies all of existence, and this substance is characterized by its inherent intelligence and creative potential.

According to Wattles, this "thinking stuff" is the source from which all things manifest. It is the substance that permeates every aspect of the world, from the physical realm to the realm of thoughts and ideas. He suggests that this substance is abundant and readily available to everyone, and by understanding and harnessing its power, individuals can shape their reality and achieve their desires.

Wattles's teachings align with the broader concept of the law of attraction, which asserts that thoughts and beliefs have the power to attract corresponding experiences and circumstances into our lives. He emphasizes the importance of aligning our thoughts and intentions with what we seek to manifest, as this harmonizes our individual consciousness with the creative substance of the universe.

The quote highlights the interconnectedness and omnipresence of this universal substance. It suggests that there is a unifying force that binds all things together, and by tapping into it, we can access the creative power of the universe.

By recognizing this interconnectedness, individuals can develop a deeper understanding of their role in shaping their reality and actively participate in the process of creation.

Wallace Wattles's insights serve as a reminder that our thoughts and beliefs are potent forces that influence our experiences. By recognizing the omnipresent thinking substance and aligning our thoughts with our desires, we can consciously create the life we envision. Through understanding and working with this universal substance, individuals can tap into their creative potential and manifest their aspirations.

# Prentice Mulford

Our thought is the unseen magnet, ever attracting its correspondence in things seen and tangible.

Prentice Mulford, an influential writer and philosopher of the New Thought movement in the late 19th century, is known for his profound teachings on the power of thoughts and the concept that "thoughts are things." Mulford believed that our thoughts possess a creative energy that can shape our experiences and influence the world around us.

Mulford's teachings centered on the idea that thoughts are not mere fleeting mental processes, but tangible forces that carry a vibration and energy. He emphasized that our thoughts have the power to manifest in our lives and attract corresponding outcomes. Positive thoughts, filled with optimism and belief, can draw positive circumstances and opportunities, while negative thoughts can bring about undesired results.

According to Mulford, the key to harnessing

the power of thoughts lies in understanding and directing our mental faculties. He believed that by consciously choosing our thoughts and cultivating positive mental states, we can create a harmonious relationship between our inner and outer world.

Mulford's teachings align with the broader concept of the law of attraction, which suggests that like attracts like. By focusing on positive thoughts, we align ourselves with the positive vibrations of the universe, attracting similar energy into our lives. Mulford's teachings were influential in shaping the understanding of the law of attraction and its practical applications.

The notion that "thoughts are things" highlights the creative potential within each individual. It reminds us of the responsibility we have to cultivate empowering thoughts and beliefs. By actively choosing positive thoughts and directing our mental energy towards our goals, we can shape our reality and bring about the experiences we desire.

Although Mulford's writings may have faded from mainstream awareness, his teachings on the power of thoughts continue to resonate with those exploring personal growth and self-improvement. The understanding that our thoughts hold the power to shape our reality serves as a reminder of the importance of mindfulness, self-awareness, and intentional thinking. It invites us to take ownership of our thoughts and consciously direct them towards creating a fulfilling and abundant life.

Napoleon Hill
Whatever Your Mind Can Conceive and Believe, It Can Achieve.

Napoleon Hill, a renowned American author and motivational speaker, is best known for his groundbreaking book "Think and Grow Rich." Within this influential work, Hill emphasizes the concept of "a burning desire" as a critical component of achieving success and realizing one's dreams.

Hill believed that a burning desire, an intense passion and unwavering commitment towards a specific goal, is the driving force behind extraordinary achievements. It is the inner flame that fuels persistence, resilience, and the ability to overcome obstacles and setbacks along the journey to success.

According to Hill, a burning desire goes beyond mere wishful thinking. It is a deep-seated, all-encompassing hunger for the attainment of a particular outcome. It creates a laser-like focus and unwavering determination that propels individuals forward, even in the face of challenges and adversity.

Hill's concept of a burning desire suggests that when one possesses a strong and clearly defined goal, coupled with an intense desire to achieve it, they tap into the infinite power of the subconscious mind. This power helps attract the necessary resources, opportunities, and people to support the realization of their dreams.

Furthermore, Hill emphasizes the importance of aligning one's burning desire with positive thoughts, beliefs, and actions. By maintaining a positive mental attitude and consistently taking inspired action towards the desired goal, individuals can harness the full potential of their burning desire and accelerate their progress.

Throughout his book, Napoleon Hill presents numerous examples of individuals who achieved great success through the power of a burning desire, including Thomas Edison, Henry Ford, and Andrew Carnegie. He stresses that a burning desire is not limited to any specific field or endeavor; it can be applied to any area of life, whether it be business, relationships, health, or personal growth.

In essence, Napoleon Hill's concept of a burning desire serves as a reminder that success starts with an intense passion and unwavering commitment towards a goal. It is a call to cultivate and nurture a powerful desire that drives us to overcome challenges, persist in the face of adversity, and take consistent action. By igniting and fueling our burning desire, we unlock our potential and pave the way to achieving remarkable outcomes in our lives.

Albert Einstein
Imagination is more important than knowledge. Knowledge is limited. Imagination encircles the world.

of relativity. While Einstein's work primarily focused on understanding the fundamental principles of the physical universe, his ideas and beliefs often touched on the concept of higher consciousness and its relationship to quantum physics.

Einstein's view of the universe went beyond the conventional understanding of a purely material existence. He saw the interconnectedness of all things and believed in a unified field of energy that underlies the fabric of reality. This perspective aligns with the principles of quantum physics, which suggests that everything in the universe, including matter and energy, is interconnected and influenced by consciousness.

Einstein's famous quote, "The most beautiful thing we can experience is the mysterious. It is the source of all true art and science," reflects his appreciation for the deeper mysteries and hidden truths of the universe. He recognized that the human mind has the capacity to delve into these mysteries and gain insight into the workings of the cosmos.

While Einstein did not explicitly delve into metaphysical or spiritual aspects of higher consciousness, his work laid the foundation for exploring the interplay between consciousness and the physical world. Quantum physics, which emerged after Einstein's time, further deepened the understanding of the interconnectedness of the observer and the observed. Quantum experiments suggest that the act of observation influences the behavior and manifestation of particles at the subatomic level.

Einstein's work and ideas paved the way for exploring the frontiers of consciousness and its role in shaping reality. Although he may not have delved extensively into the spiritual or metaphysical aspects of higher consciousness, his work in physics has opened doors for further inquiry and exploration into the nature of consciousness and its relationship to the physical world.

Einstein's contributions continue to inspire scientists, philosophers, and spiritual seekers to explore the realms of consciousness beyond the confines of the material world. His work invites us to question our understanding of reality, to expand our consciousness, and to embrace the profound mysteries that lie at the intersection of science and spirituality.

Carl Jung

Who looks outside, dreams; who looks inside, awakes.

Carl Jung, the influential Swiss psychiatrist and psychoanalyst, made significant contributions to our understanding of the human psyche. Three key concepts associated with Jung's work are collective consciousness, archetypes, and synchronicity.

Jung introduced the concept of collective consciousness, which refers to the shared reservoir of human experiences, knowledge, and symbols that are inherited and exist within the collective unconscious. According to Jung, this collective consciousness shapes our thoughts, beliefs, and behaviors, and influences our collective cultural, social, and spiritual dynamics. It is the source of universal themes and patterns that are found across cultures, such as the hero's journey or the mother figure archetype.

Archetypes, another fundamental concept in

Jung's work, are universal patterns or symbols that reside within the collective unconscious. They represent fundamental aspects of the human experience, such as the wise old man, the nurturing mother, or the trickster. These archetypes serve as primordial blueprints that shape our perceptions, emotions, and behaviors, often operating at an unconscious level. By recognizing and integrating these archetypal energies, individuals can gain a deeper understanding of themselves and the world around them.

Synchronicity is a concept that Jung coined to describe meaningful coincidences that occur without a causal explanation. According to Jung, these synchronistic events are not random occurrences but rather meaningful connections between the inner and outer world. They suggest a deeper interconnectedness and purposeful unfolding of events beyond the limitations of linear cause and effect. Synchronicity points to the existence of a meaningful and intelligent organizing principle in the universe, where the inner world of thoughts and symbols influences the external world.

Jung's exploration of collective consciousness, archetypes, and synchronicity revolutionized our understanding of the human psyche and its relationship to the broader world. His ideas offer a holistic framework that goes beyond individual psychology to include cultural, spiritual, and transpersonal dimensions. They invite us to explore the depths of our own psyche, recognize the universal patterns that shape our experiences, and appreciate the mysterious and meaningful connections that unfold in our lives. Jung's work continues to inspire individuals in fields ranging from psychology to spirituality, offering insights into the profound interplay between the individual and the collective, and the potential for self-discovery and growth.

Nikola Tesla
If you want to find the secrets of the universe, think in terms of energy, frequency, and vibration.

Nikola Tesla, the brilliant inventor and electrical engineer, is known for his groundbreaking contributions to the field of science and technology. While Tesla's work spanned various areas, his fascination with numbers and their significance is evident in his exploration of the 3, 6, 9 number sequence.

Tesla believed that numbers held profound significance and that certain numbers carried particular power and resonance. The 3, 6, 9 sequence held a special place in his understanding of the universe. According to Tesla, these numbers represented fundamental frequencies and vibrations that are integral to the fabric of reality.

In Tesla's view, the number 9 stood out as the most powerful number in the sequence. He considered it to be the key to unlocking the secrets of the universe. Tesla believed that by understanding and harnessing the frequencies and vibrations associated with the number 9, one could tap into the fundamental forces that shape existence.

The significance of the number 9 in Tesla's thinking can be understood in terms of numerology and its association with completion, wholeness, and spiritual enlightenment. It is often seen as a number of wisdom and spiritual attainment.

From a scientific perspective, the number 9 can be linked to mathematical patterns and harmonics. For example, when the digits of multiples of 9 are added together, they always reduce to 9. This pattern suggests a self-referencing and self-sustaining quality that resonates with the concept of wholeness and completion.

Tesla's belief in the power of numbers and their connection to frequencies and vibrations aligns with the understanding that everything in the universe is fundamentally energy in motion. Frequencies and vibrations underlie the manifestation of physical reality. By harmonizing with the vibrations associated with certain numbers, it is believed that one can align with the energetic patterns that shape the desired reality.

While the specifics of Tesla's beliefs regarding the 3, 6, 9 number sequence and the power of 9 may be subject to interpretation, his fascination with the significance of numbers reflects his deep appreciation for the underlying harmony and order in the universe. It invites us to explore the interconnectedness of mathematics, frequencies, vibrations, and the manifestation of our desired reality.

Charles Haanel
I am whole, perfect, strong, powerful, loving, harmonious, and happy.

Charles F. Haanel was an American author and businessman who gained recognition for his influential work, "The Master Key System." Published in 1912, the book remains a cornerstone of the self-help and personal development genre.

"The Master Key System" is a comprehensive program that provides readers with a practical guide to achieving success and personal growth. Haanel's work revolves around the idea that our thoughts and beliefs shape our reality, and by understanding and harnessing the power of our mind, we can unlock our full potential.

The book consists of 24 lessons, each designed to impart key principles and techniques for self-mastery. Haanel explores various concepts, including visualization, concentration, affirmation, and the power of gratitude. He emphasizes the importance of aligning one's thoughts and beliefs with their desired goals and maintaining a positive mental attitude.

One of the key ideas in "The Master Key System" is that the mind operates as a creative force, capable of attracting and manifesting the desired outcomes. Haanel presents a systematic approach to utilizing the power of the mind through disciplined thinking and focused intention.

His teachings have had a lasting impact on the field of personal development, influencing subsequent authors and thought leaders, including Napoleon Hill and Rhonda Byrne. Haanel's emphasis on the power of thought and its connection to success has resonated with countless individuals seeking to improve their lives.

"The Master Key System" encourages readers to take responsibility for their thoughts, develop mental clarity, and cultivate positive beliefs. By applying the principles outlined in the book, individuals can gain greater control over their lives, tap into their innate potential, and create a more fulfilling and abundant reality.

Charles F. Haanel's work continues to be celebrated for its holistic approach to personal transformation. Through "The Master Key System," he offers readers a roadmap to unlock their inner power and create lasting positive change in all areas of life.

Sadhguru
The quality of your life is determined by how peaceful & joyful you are within yourself.

Sadhguru, whose birth name is Jaggi Vasudev, is a renowned spiritual leader, yogi, and author. He is widely respected for his profound wisdom, insightful teachings, and ability to bring spirituality into practical aspects of life. Sadhguru has dedicated his life to fostering inner transformation and guiding individuals towards realizing their full potential.

Sadhguru is the founder of the Isha Foundation, a non-profit organization dedicated to promoting well-being and spiritual growth. The foundation offers a variety of programs and initiatives focused on yoga, meditation, environmental conservation, and social outreach.

One of Sadhguru's key contributions is the introduction of the Inner Engineering program, which aims to provide individuals with tools and techniques for inner well-being and self-realization. Through a combination of yoga, meditation, and mindfulness practices, Inner Engineering offers a holistic approach to personal growth and transformation.

Sadhguru's teachings emphasize the importance of self-awareness, self-discovery, and aligning one's life with natural laws and universal principles. He encourages individuals to take responsibility for their own well-being, both on an individual and global scale. Sadhguru's approach is pragmatic, blending ancient wisdom with contemporary insights, making it accessible to people from all walks of life.

Sadhguru is also known for his environmental activism and commitment to sustainable living. He initiated the Rally for Rivers campaign, which aimed to raise awareness about the critical condition of India's rivers and promote the revitalization and conservation of these vital water resources.

Through his books, public talks, and online presence, Sadhguru has reached millions of people worldwide, inspiring them to embark on a journey of self-exploration and personal transformation. His teachings encompass a broad range of topics, including spirituality, relationships, health, and success, providing guidance for individuals seeking a more meaningful and purposeful life.

Sadhguru's influence extends beyond the realm of spirituality. His pragmatic and inclusive approach has resonated with people from diverse backgrounds, making him a sought-after speaker at various forums, including international conferences and academic institutions.

Overall, Sadhguru's teachings and contributions have had a profound impact on the lives of countless individuals, guiding them towards inner growth, well-being, and a deeper sense of connection with themselves and the world around them.

Matthew McConaughey
Guilt and regret kills many a man
before their time.

Matthew McConaughey, the acclaimed American actor, is not only known for his talent on the screen but also for his unique philosophy of life. Throughout his career, McConaughey has shared profound insights and personal experiences that reflect his distinctive perspective on living a fulfilling and authentic life.

McConaughey's philosophy can be summarized by his mantra, "Just keep livin'." This simple yet powerful phrase embodies his approach to life, emphasizing the importance of staying present, embracing challenges, and continuously seeking personal growth and self-improvement.

He encourages individuals to embrace uncertainty, take risks, and maintain a sense of curiosity and wonder. McConaughey believes that life's most valuable experiences lie beyond our comfort zones, and by pushing our boundaries, we open ourselves up to new opportunities and personal transformation.

Authenticity is a key aspect of McConaughey's philosophy. He advocates for staying true to oneself and honoring individuality, even in the face of societal pressures or expectations. He encourages people to trust their instincts, follow their passions, and create their own paths in life.

McConaughey also emphasizes the importance of gratitude and finding joy in the present moment. He encourages individuals to appreciate the journey rather than solely focusing on the destination. According to him, true fulfillment comes from embracing the present and finding beauty in the ordinary aspects of life.

In his book, "Greenlights," McConaughey shares personal anecdotes, life lessons, and reflections on his own journey. He provides insights into his unconventional path to success, highlighting the importance of perseverance, resilience, and self-belief.

Beyond his professional achievements, McConaughey's philosophy of life has resonated with many individuals who seek a more authentic and meaningful existence. His unique blend of wisdom, optimism, and zest for life serves as an inspiration to embrace each moment, stay true to oneself, and continuously evolve on the journey of self-discovery.

Through his words and actions, Matthew McConaughey encourages others to live with purpose, embrace challenges, and maintain a positive outlook, ultimately inspiring individuals to find their own definition of success and fulfillment.

***Closing thoughts from a flow moment on a beach in paradise on a coast in Brasil where I suddenly find myself building a niche existence…***

Life is about finding your rhythm. It's about going with your flow and the flow to go with your flow and understand how to flow and when you don't know what is flow and where is flow and what to know to flow.

That is when you must go. That is when you must move. Your feet, your body, your spirit, your mind will follow if you just move, if you walk and talk, if you speak with the world around you, if you speak with yourself, if you meditate, if you concentrate your mind on something that is simmering in the back of its hind legs, that want to sprawl forward and jump like a kangaroo into a new you.

That is where you'll find movement, flow, magic, unfurling potential and possibility, like a beautiful spinnaker in front of a great ship. That is your ship that if you don't know it's, yours. And if you don't know it exists, you can never be captain of.

We're out here on the high seas. Yes. All of us. Navigators in time and space. In a heart, in a mind, in a soul and a body. In a time, within a time, in a mind, within a mind, conscience, unconscious, we are all here in both places it is up to us to become the sculptors of all reality to understand that we are here to sculpt it, to be it, to become it, to live it, to drive it, to know it, to be it and.

One day to magically think it into existence and know that it is through our thinking, that it is through our being that that such thing has been created. And that is the greatest gift that God has given us all the opportunity to understand this beautiful mystery, the opportunity to flow inside of God's glow.

That is life. That is the beautiful and furling spinnaker in front of all of our ships. And it is up to us to find it, to let it unfurl and to follow it, my dear friends, to discover that beautiful pearl inside of that shell of ours that we often hide inside of.

That is the great mystery. That is the great adventure. And that is the great desafio (Portuguese for challenge). That is our quest. So must we take this quest, put it in our heart, wear it like a shield and go into everyday knowing that we are warriors of light and we are here to stand strong, and through it all become light.

Amen. Amen. Amen.

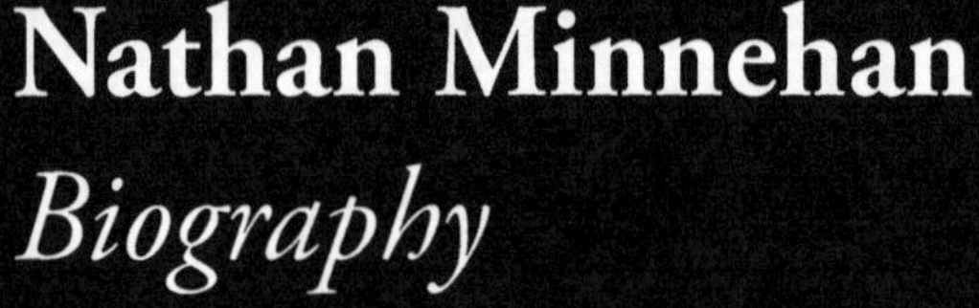
Nathan Minnehan
Biography

As a spiritual serial entrepreneur with several successful ventures, Nathan Minnehan continues to cherish the process of transitioning from the moment of aha to the triumphant hallelujah of accomplishment. Minnehan's entrepreneurial journey commenced in 2010, driven by the belief in having something valuable to share with the world, a sentiment that persists to this day. With a portfolio of 18 thriving ventures, ranging from small micro brands to a company that generated three-quarters of a million dollars within the first three months of its existence, Minnehan remains actively involved in their operation.

Dedicated to assisting high performers in unlocking their greatness, manifesting their mojo, and fulfilling their higher purpose, Minnehan is committed to supporting others in achieving abundance in their pursuits.

Nathan speaks fluent Czech, Spanish, Portuguese, and English. His yearning to define the spiritual forces assisting him in propelling through purpose in each venture has been and continues to be the burning desire inside of him. 3,6,9 Secrets is merely a reflection back on the unique sets of not so common tools that Minnehan believes have made all of the difference in his personal pursuit of success and the fulfilling of his vision for a thriving life.

If you or someone you know would like to transform your life and move into a quantum plane of living and thriving then Minnehan is your man. Not only does Nathan work one on one with clients to download their roadmap for transformation, but he and his team then also execute on bringing your compelling new vision to reality. From birthing brands, to crafting looks with luxury couture clothing, Minnehan's team does it seamlessly. As the owner of Authortobe.com, he also helps amazing individuals become authors and solidify their purpose, and bandwidth for focus and impact in their life and legacy.

**To book a session with Nathan, visit:**

www.nathanontap.com

**Or simply navigate to**

www.mastermaker.global

**and get started executing on your higher purpose today!**

READY TO BECOME AN AUTHOR?
Looking for a hand?
AUTHOR TOBE
We'd love to help!
VISIT US AT
WWW.AUTHORTOBE.COM

www.ingramcontent.com/pod-product-compliance
Lightning Source LLC
La Vergne TN
LVHW020519100826
845148LV00010B/1286

* 9 7 9 8 9 5 0 4 4 4 0 1 2 *